Walter Angonese

Vorwort

Der Begriff «Baukunst» sagt es: Die Architektur kann als eine Disziplin gelten, die nahe der Kunst steht. Denn eigentlich ist Walter Angonese kein Architekt im traditionellen Sinn. Eher ist er ein Bildhauer, ein Raumkünstler. Er bedient sich der Architektur gleichsam als Künstler, und er demonstriert, wie die Architektur hin zu einer freieren Kunst geführt werden kann. So überwindet die Architektur bei Walter Angonese – nicht selten mit List – Konventionen, Baugesetze, erstarrte Traditionen.

Der vorliegende Band zeigt 24 Bauten und Bauprojekte von ihm. Jeder und jedes ist mit nur einem oder zwei prägnanten Bildern und den wichtigsten Grundrissen oder Schnitten dargestellt. Um ihren Reichtum zu erfahren, müssen die Bauten schliesslich besichtigt sein. Der begleitende Text beschreibt präzise den architektonischen Willen, der hinter den inspirierten vielschichtigen Bauwerken steht. Und ebenso lesen wir, welche Leidenschaft bis hin zur Verschmelzung der Architektur mit seiner Aufgabe und seinem Ort und zum starken architektonischen Ausdruck die Bauten beseelt. Die Kategorien der Architektur sind immer lesbar: der Innenraum, die äussere Figur, die Einbettung in die Topografie, die Funktionalität, der Bezug zur Landschaft, zur Historie, zum gesellschaftlichen «Gedächtnis». Zu Beginn des Bandes sind als Collage einige geistige und ikonografische Inspirationsquellen des Architekten – gleichsam der Stoff für seine Architektur – spielerisch angedeutet.

Das in Italien liegende Südtirol befindet sich an einem ganz anderen Ort Europas als etwa London, Amsterdam, Berlin oder München. Und das macht schliesslich diese Reihe *De aedibus international* aus: die Inspirationen, die architektonischen Kulturen einzelner Architekten in Europa zu dokumentieren und zusammenzuführen. Um zu zeigen, welche kraftvollen, liebenswerten architektonischen Blüten auf dem europäischen Kontinent blühen. Es ist gleichsam ein Gespräch der Architekten über die Landesgrenzen und Kulturräume hinweg.

Heinz Wirz, Luzern im Juli 2016

Foreword

As the phrase "art of building" expresses, architecture can be regarded as a discipline that is close to art. Actually, Walter Angonese is not an architect in a traditional sense. He is more a sculptor, a spatial artist. He draws from architecture as an artist and demonstrates how architecture can be brought closer to a freer art. In this way, the architecture of Walter Angonese often has a craftiness in overcoming conventions, regulations and stilted traditions.

This volume presents 24 buildings and construction projects. Each is only presented using one or two concise images and the most important floor plans or sectional views. After all, to experience their wealth, one must visit the buildings themselves. The accompanying text describes precisely the architectural will that drives the inspired, multifaceted buildings forward. We also read about the passion with which he merges the architecture with its task and location, enthusing the buildings with a powerful architectural expression. The categories of architecture are always legible: the interior, the external figure, embedding into the topography, functionalism, and a reference to the landscape, history and social "memory". The book begins with a number of the architect's iconographic sources of inspiration that also provide material for his architecture, presented as a collage with a hint of playfulness.

Italy's South Tyrol is a completely different European location compared to London, Amsterdam, Berlin or Munich. That is what distinguishes the *De aedibus international* series, with its aim of documenting and bringing together the inspiration and architectural cultures of individual architects in Europe. It reveals what powerful, admirable architectural flowers bloom on the continent of Europe. It is like a dialogue between the architects across national boundaries and cultural regions.

Heinz Wirz, Lucerne, July 2016

14 De aedibus international

Walter Angonese
Kaltern/Caldaro

Quart Verlag Luzern

Walter Angonese
14. Band der Reihe De aedibus international / Volume 14 of the series De aedibus international

Herausgeber / Edited by: Heinz Wirz, Luzern
Konzept/Concept: Walter Angonese, Kaltern/Caldaro; Arno Ritter, Innsbruck;
Jacopo Vantini, Padua/Padova; Heinz Wirz
Projektleitung / Project management: Quart Verlag, Antonia Wirz
Textbeitrag / Article by: Arno Ritter, Innsbruck
Objekttexte / Project descriptions: Walter Angonese, Kaltern/Caldaro
Vorwort/Foreword: Heinz Wirz
Übersetzung Deutsch–Englisch / English translation: Benjamin Liebelt, Berlin
Textlektorat Deutsch / Text editing (German): Mirjam Seifert-Waibel, Hamburg
Textlektorat Deutsch (Vorwort) / Text editing (German, Foreword): Kirsten Rachowiak, München
Fotos/Photos: Günter Richard Wett, Innsbruck; ausser/except: Arno Gisinger, Paris S./p. 13;
Jürgen Eheim, Brixen/Bressanone S./p. 16/17, 53, 64 l, 65 r; Paolo Riolzi, Mailand/Milano
S./p. 35, 36, 37; Nikolaus Schletterer, Innsbruck S./p. 65 l; Marco Riebler, Salzburg S./p. 68;
Walter Angonese, Kaltern/Caldaro S./p. 69
Grafische Umsetzung / Graphic design: Quart Verlag, Antonia Wirz
Druck/Printing: DZA Druckerei zu Altenburg GmbH

ISBN 978-3-03761-121-0

Quart Verlag GmbH
Denkmalstrasse 2, CH-6006 Luzern
books@quart.ch, www.quart.ch

Manfred Alois Mayr, Fontana dei libri, Roma, 2016

S P Q R

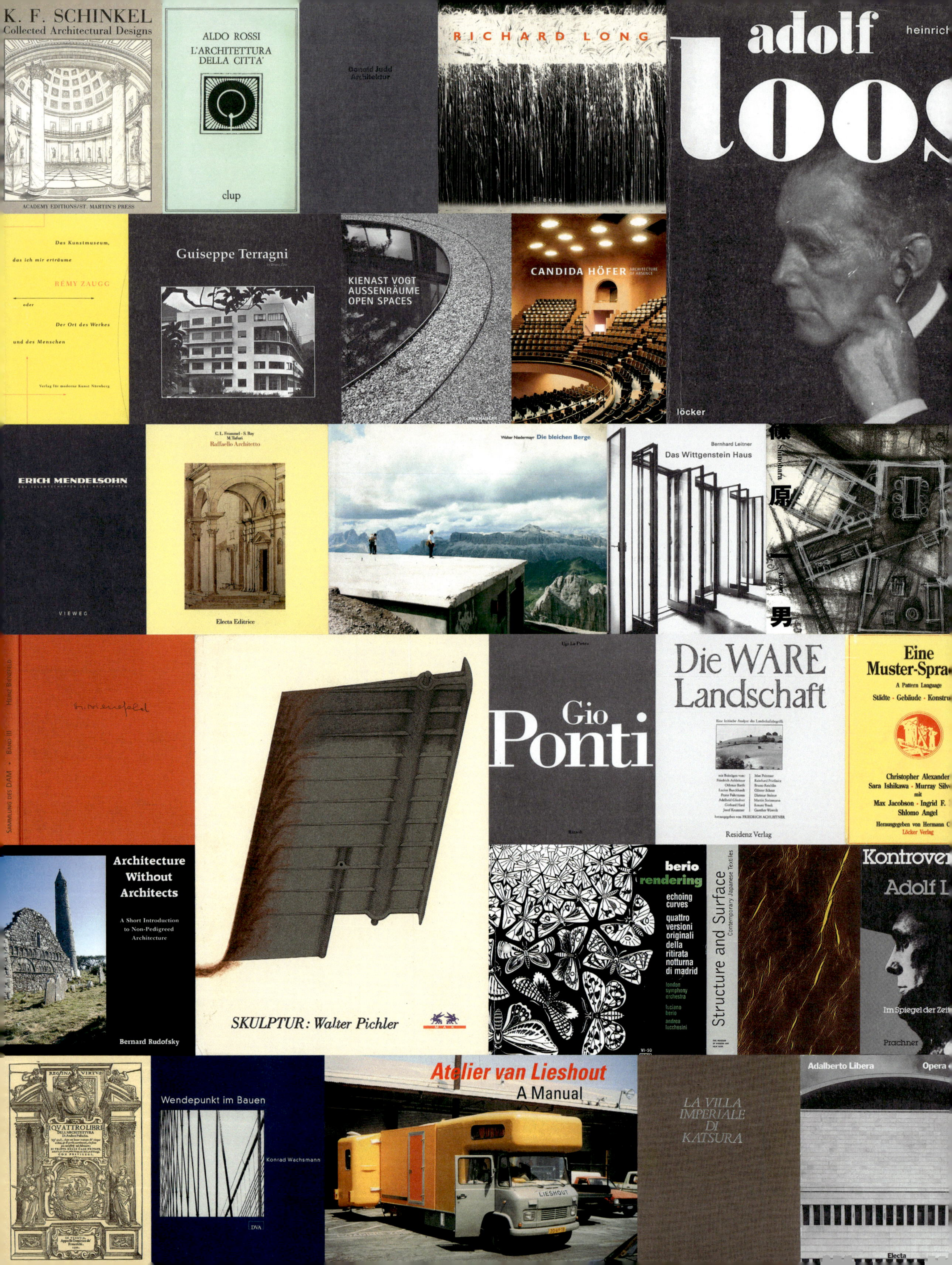
K. F. SCHINKEL
Collected Architectural Designs
ACADEMY EDITIONS/ST. MARTIN'S PRESS
ALDO ROSSI
L'ARCHITETTURA DELLA CITTA'
clup
Donald Judd Architektur
RICHARD LONG
Electa
adolf
heinrich
loos
löcker
Das Kunstmuseum,
das ich mir erträume
RÉMY ZAUGG
oder
Der Ort des Werkes
und des Menschen
Verlag für moderne Kunst Nürnberg
Guiseppe Terragni
KIENAST VOGT
AUSSENRÄUME
OPEN SPACES
CANDIDA HÖFER
ARCHITECTURE OF ABSENCE
ERICH MENDELSOHN
VIEWEG
C. L. Frommel · S. Ray
M. Tafuri
Raffaello Architetto
Electa Editrice
Walter Niedermayr Die bleichen Berge
Bernhard Leitner
Das Wittgenstein Haus
篠原一男
Shinohara Kazuo
SAMMLUNG DES DAM · BAND III · HEINZ BIENEFELD
Gio Ponti
Die WARE Landschaft
Residenz Verlag
Eine Muster-Spra
A Pattern Language
Städte · Gebäude · Konstru
Christopher Alexander
Sara Ishikawa · Murray Silve
mit
Max Jacobson · Ingrid F.
Shlomo Angel
Löcker Verlag
Architecture Without Architects
A Short Introduction to Non-Pedigreed Architecture
Bernard Rudofsky
SKULPTUR: Walter Pichler
berio
rendering
echoing curves
quattro versioni originali della ritirata notturna di madrid
london symphony orchestra
luciano berio
andrea lucchesini
Structure and Surface
Contemporary Japanese Textiles
Kontrover
Adolf L
Im Spiegel der Zeit
Prachner
I QUATTRO LIBRI DELL'ARCHITETTURA
Wendepunkt im Bauen
Konrad Wachsmann
DVA
Atelier van Lieshout
A Manual
LIESHOUT
LA VILLA IMPERIALE DI KATSURA
Adalberto Libera
Opera
Electa

Luk ap

Weingut Hofstätter

Hofstätter winery

Ausführung/Construction: 1996–1998
Bauherrschaft/Client: Weingut Josef Hofstätter
Architektur/Architecture: Walter Angonese, Zeno Bampi, Markus Scherer
Mitarbeiter/Collaborators: Sanja Balta Radic, Silvia Boday, Günther Franzelin, Natalia Houlgin
Bauingenieur / Structural engineer: Sergio Cesare
Künstlerische Intervention / Artistic intervention: Martin Pohl

Am Anfang stand ein reiner Fassadenwettbewerb, dem Bauherrn wurde aber bald klar, dass der Lagerturm einer Weinkellerei mit hohen qualitativen und funktionalen Ansprüchen wohl ganzheitlicher gedacht werden musste. Der Lagerturm des Weingutes Hofstätter, eingespannt zwischen einem barocken Palais und dem 1492 errichteten spätgotischen Kirchturm von Tramin, entwickelt sich auf einem relativ engen Grundstück über fünf Geschosse. Der Anspruch an eine optimale Wärmedämmung und eine semantisch orientierte Herangehensweise haben zu einer in mehreren Schichten aufgebauten Lösung geführt, die aus massiven Vollziegelwänden mit Heraklitdämmung und Hinterlüftung sowie einer 4 Zentimeter starken massiven Eichenholzfassade besteht. Das Gebäude weist bis zum obersten Geschoss keine sichtbaren Öffnungen auf – nur Lüftungselemente gewährleisten einen Luftaustausch –, während im letzten Geschoss ein Verkostungsraum und eine Loggia untergebracht sind, deren Beschattung über Schiebeelemente erfolgt.

To begin with there was simply a facade competition, but the client soon realised that the storage tower for a winery with high demands in terms of quality and function had to be conceived in a more holistic way. Inserted between the Baroque palais and the late Gothic church tower of Termeno dating back to 1492, the storage tower for the Hofstätter winery develops over five storeys on a relatively narrow plot. The requirement of ideal heat insulation and a semantically orientated approach led to a solution based on several layers, consisting of solid brick walls with Heraklith insulation and back-ventilation, as well as a 4-centimetre solid oak wood façade. Up to the top floor, the building has no visible openings – only ventilation units ensure the exchange of air – while a tasting room and a loggia are accommodated on the top floor, with sliding shutters providing protection from the sun.

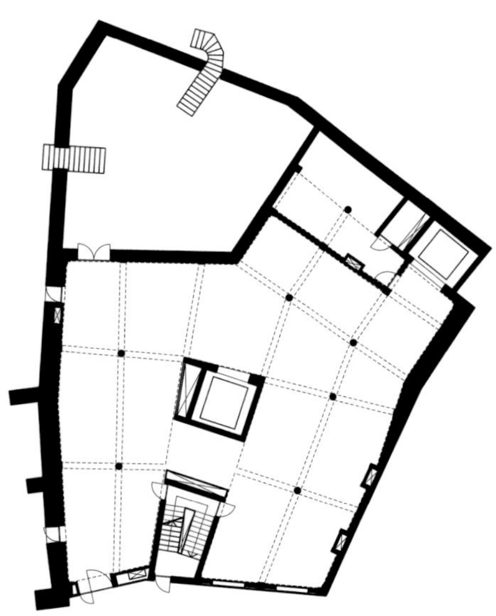

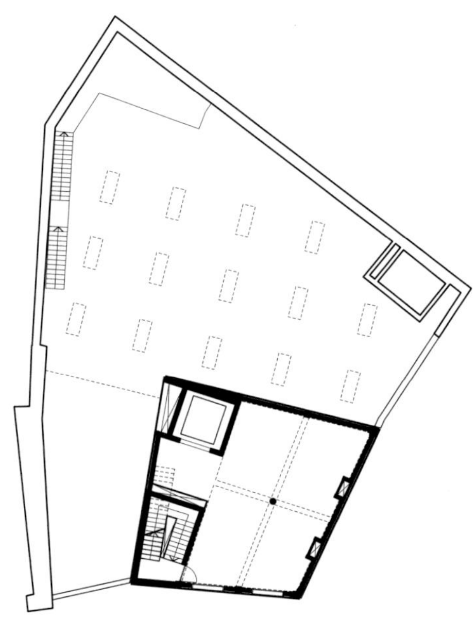

10 m

Josefsburg, Festung Kufstein

Josefsburg, Kufstein Fortress

Ausführung/Construction:
1998–1999
Bauherrschaft/Client:
Top City GmbH, Kufstein
Architektur/Architecture:
Walter Angonese, Andreas Egger, Markus Scherer
Mitarbeiter/Collaborators: Sanja Balta Radic, Verena Hofer-Capaldo
Bauingenieur / Structural engineers: Pro Statik, Walter Speiser, Kufstein
Künstlerische Intervention / Artistic intervention: Martin Pohl

Die Josefsburg, die westlichste Bastion der Festungsanlage Kufstein, war in einem desolaten Zustand und bedurfte einer dringenden Restaurierung. Der Innenhof wies ein enormes Potenzial für Veranstaltungen auf, das die Stadt Kufstein nutzen wollte. Neben der konservativen Restaurierung der Kasematten mit der Implantierung von Infrastrukturen wie Fenstern und neuen Böden wurden mehrere Rampen und Treppenanlagen errichtet und im östlichen Bereich ein in Stahlbau ausgeführter Mehrzweckraum im Erdgeschoss und eine grosse Nasszellenanlage im Kellergeschoss konzipiert. Neben der Sanierung der Kasematten – man besann sich auf massive Lehmabdichtungen – kennzeichnen die in angerostetem Stahl ausgeführten neuen Bauteile die Interventionen an der Josefsburg. Jahre später wurde der grosse Innenhof durch die Stadt Kufstein mit einem massstäblich überdimensionierten Schutzdach für Veranstaltungen versehen, das die subtilen Interventionen der vorhergehenden Restaurierung und Adaptierung in Mitleidenschaft gezogen hat.

Josefsburg, the western-most bastion of Kufstein Fortress, was in a dilapidated condition and required urgent restoration. The interior courtyard has enormous potential for events, which the City of Kufstein wished to exploit. In addition to the conservative restoration of the casemates and the installation of infrastructures such as windows and new flooring, several ramps and staircases were also constructed. In the eastern section, a steel multifunctional hall and a large sanitary facility were conceived in the basement. Aside from the renovated casemates – which exclusively use clay sealing – the newly added building elements in pre-rusted steel characterise the Josefsburg interventions. Years later, the City of Kufstein added an oversized protective roof to the large interior courtyard in order to hold events there, which had a negative effect on the subtle interventions of the previous restoration and adaptation.

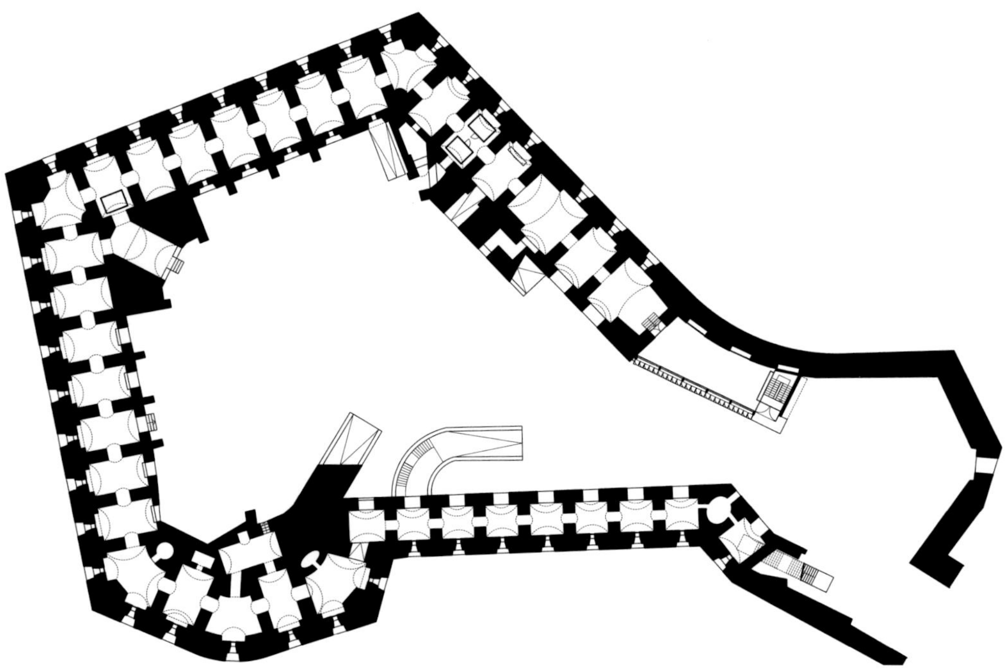

Schloss Tirol

Tyrol Castle

Ausführung/Construction: 1993–2002; 2012–2014
Bauherrschaft/Client: Autonome Provinz Bozen Südtirol
Architektur/Architecture: Walter Angonese, Klaus Hellweger, Markus Scherer
Mitarbeiter/Collaborators: Sanja Balta Radic, Alessia Carlotto, Yvonne Garbukas, Anja Richter
Bauingenieur / Structural engineers: Roberto Beneduce, Hartmut Theiner
Künstlerische Intervention / Artistic intervention: Gottfried Bechtold, Elisabeth Hölzl, Kurt Lanthaler, Walter Niedermayr, Carmen Tartarotti
Kuratorenteam / Curator team: Elisabeth Baumgartner, Siegfried De Rachewiltz, Benno Erhard, Barbara Gabrieli, Christiane Ganner, Hans Heiss, Silvia Höller, Julia Hörmann, Carl Kraus, Paula Mair, Giorgio Mezzalira, Petra Paolazzi, Marion Piffer Damiani
Grafik / Graphic design: Circus, Büro für Kommunikation und Gestaltung (Kurt Hoeretzeder, Andreas Schett, Andrea Senfter)

Die Stammburg der Grafen von Tirol besitzt eine facettenreiche Geschichte. Mitte der 1990er Jahre beschloss die Südtiroler Landesregierung, dort das kultur- und landesgeschichtliche Museum zu eröffnen. Neben zahlreichen konservatorischen Massnahmen wurde ein Museumskonzept erstellt, das sich in einer stark am thematischen Konzept orientierten Museumsarchitektur niederschlug, die einerseits mit den sehr unterschiedlichen Räumen umgehen musste und andererseits die kuratorischen Vorgaben in jeweils spezifische Raumstimmungen umsetzten wollte. Am markantesten lässt sich der Dialog zwischen Bestand und Museumskonzept am Bergfried ablesen, der erst zu Beginn des 20. Jahrhunderts vollendet auch unter denkmalpflegerischen Überlegungen die Möglichkeit bot, ein eigenständiges räumliches Konzept zuzulassen. Mit 20 Schwerpunktthemen und entsprechenden Vertiefungsebenen wird in dem 20 Meter hohen Innenraum die Geschichte Südtirols im 20. Jahrhundert erzählt.

The ancestral castle of the Count of Tyrol has had a varied history. In the mid-1990s, the state government of South Tyrol decided to open its cultural-historical museum there. In addition to numerous conservational measures, a museum concept was developed that resulted in an architecture that was strongly orientated towards the thematic concept, making it necessary to deal with highly contrasting rooms and also implement the exhibiting requirements in the specific individual room atmospheres. This dialogue between the existing structures and the museum concept can be seen most strikingly in the dungeon, which was only completed at the beginning of the 20th century and, applying monument preservation considerations, offered the chance to allow an autonomous spatial concept. The 20-metre high interior space presents the history of South Tyrol in the 20th century, including 20 focus themes and accompanying in-depth presentation levels.

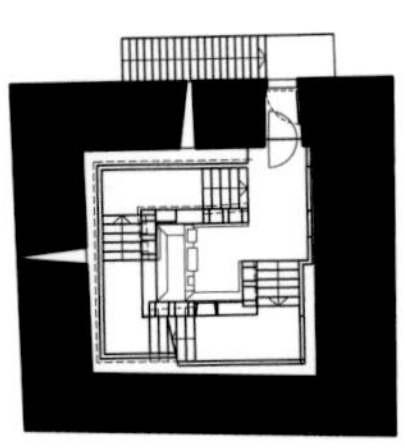

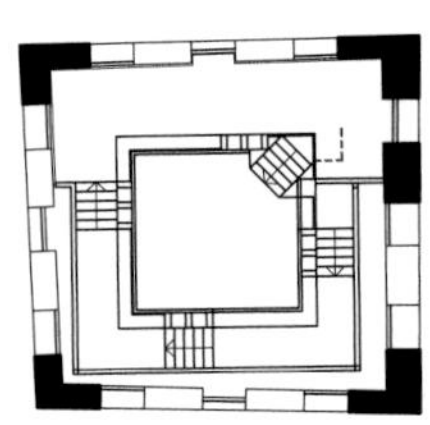

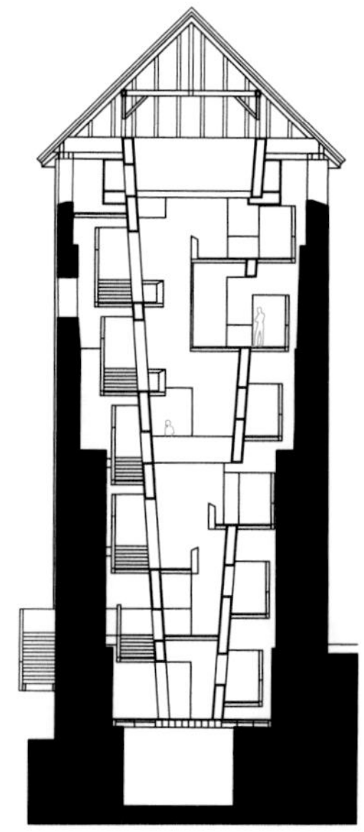

10 m

„Die Treue siegt!"
"La fedeltà vince!"
1943

Weingut Manincor

Manincor winery

Ausführung/Construction:
2001–2004
Bauherrschaft/Client: Michael Graf Goëss-Enzenberg
Architektur/Architecture:
Walter Angonese, Rainer Köberl
Mitarbeiter/Collaborator:
Silvia Boday
Bauingenieur / Structural engineers:
Ingenieurteam Bergmeister
Künstlerische Intervention / Artistic intervention: Manfred Alois Mayr, Walter Niedermayr (Buch/Book), Erik Steinbrecher, Josef Trattner

An diesem 1608 errichteten Ansitz oberhalb des Kalterer Sees sollte für die Gesamtproduktion des Gräflich Enzenberg'schen Weingutes ein neuer Weinkeller errichtet werden, wobei die historischen Keller im neuen Konzept zu berücksichtigen waren. Das Projekt nutzt die Topografie des Ortes und positioniert sich grösstenteils unterirdisch an der Hangkante der Rebberge. Nur die Haupteinfahrt, ein Servicezugang für Traktoren und der Verkostungsraum ragen ein wenig aus der Erde heraus. Als *missing link* zwischen dem über 35 000 Kubikmeter grossen neuen Keller und dem historischen Bestand fungiert der Verkaufspavillon, der eine tektonische Herausforderung darstellt: Holzstützen tragen ein Betondach. Das vorwiegend unterirdische Gebäude wurde in Beton ausgeführt, Passerellen und Tore in Cortenstahl, der mit Leinöl fixiert wurde. Auf ein ausgewogenes Gleichgewicht zwischen Funktion und Architektur wurde während des gesamten Planungsprozesses grosser Wert gelegt. Künstlerische Interventionen von Erik Steinbrecher und Manfred Alois Mayr ergänzen und verstärken die Grundstimmung.

A new wine cellar was to be constructed at the site of a lodge built above Lake Kaltern in 1608, to accommodate the entire production of the Gräflich Enzenberg'sche winery, while taking the historical cellars into account in the new concept. The project uses the topography of the location and positions itself mainly underground on the edge of the vineyards' sloping terrain. Only the main entrance, a service access for tractors and the tasting room protrude a little above the ground. The sales pavilion acts as a kind of missing link between the new cellar, with a size of over 35,000 cubic metres, and the historical existing structures. It represents a tectonic challenge: timber columns support a concrete ceiling. The mainly underground building is made of concrete, while the passerelles and gates consist of Corten steel that was fixed with linseed oil. A balance between function and architecture was a high priority throughout the entire planning process. Artistic interventions by Erik Steinbrecher and Manfred Alois Mayr complement and enhance the underlying atmosphere.

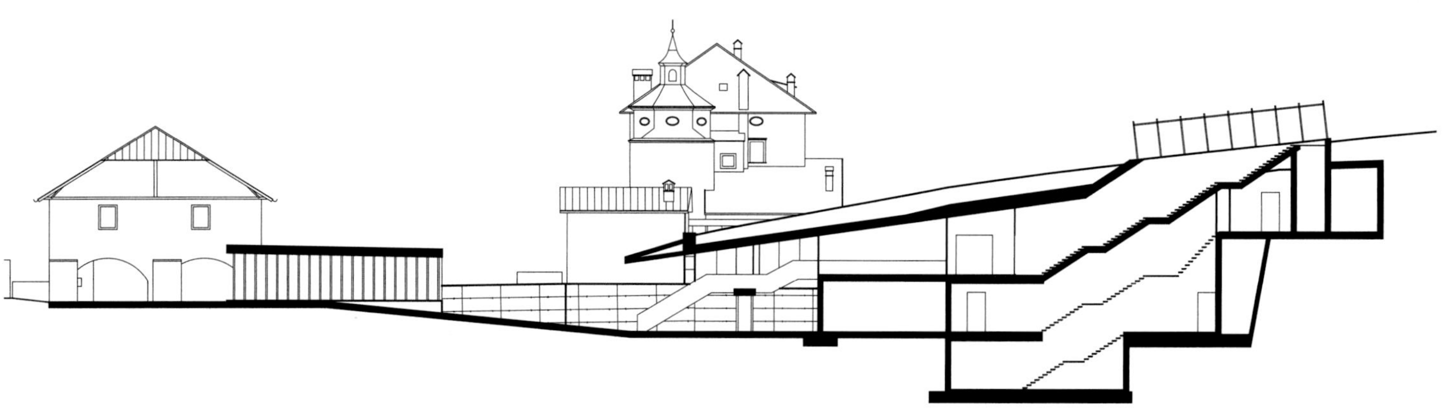

10 m

MANINCOR

Arbeiterhaus, Verwaltung Graf Enzenberg

Employees' house, Count Enzenberg administration

Ausführung/Construction: 2001–2003
Bauherrschaft/Client: Michael Graf Goëss-Enzenberg
Architektur/Architecture: Walter Angonese
Mitarbeiter/Collaborator: Silvia Boday
Bauingenieur / Structural engineers: Ingenieurteam Bergmeister
Künstlerische Intervention / Artistic intervention: Andrea M. Varesco

Auf dem Gelände der ehemaligen Enzenbergischen Ziegelfabrik in Siebeneich bei Terlan wurde ein Low-Budget-Wohnhaus für sechs langjährige landwirtschaftliche Mitarbeiter mit Familien errichtet. Mit 70 bis 100 Quadratmetern sind die Wohungsgrundrisse grosszügig und familienfreundlich bemessen. Das Gelände befindet sich im lösbodenhaltigen Bereich des Etschtales, was dazu veranlasste, die Gebäudefundamente nur in zwei Bereichen zu gründen und darauf ein brückenähnliches Gebäude in Stahl/Stahlbeton-Mischtechnik zu errichten. Auf zwei eingeschossigen, als landwirtschaftliche Lager genutzten Kuben ruht ein dreigeschossiger Baukörper, der im Erdgeschoss einen grosszügig überdachten platzähnlichen Raum bildet, welcher von den Bewohnern für gemeinschaftliche Aktivitäten genutzt wird. Nach Süden hin sind den Wohnungen Loggien vorgesetzt, während nach Osten, Westen und Norden der Bau fast hermetisch mit rotem Wellblech verkleidet ist.

On the grounds of the former Enzenberg brickyard in Siebeneich near Terlano, a low-budget house was built for six long-standing agricultural employees and their families. The floor plans of the apartments with sizes of 70 to 100 square metres are spacious and family-friendly. The grounds are situated in the Löss-soil area of the Adige Valley, so it was decided to lay the foundations only in two places and build a bridge-like building on top of it using a mixed steel and reinforced concrete technique. A three-storey building is supported by two single-storey cubes that had previously been used for agricultural storage. On the ground floor, a spacious, covered square-like area is created and used by the residents for communal activities. Towards the south, the apartments have loggias in front of them, while to the east, west and north, the building is almost hermetically clad in red corrugated metal.

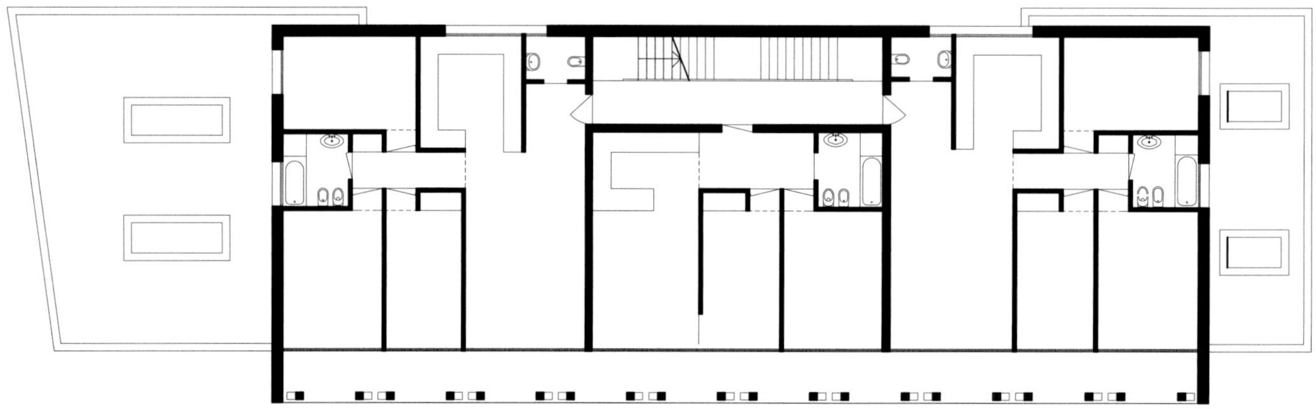

5 m

Barriquekeller, Kellerei St. Michael Eppan

Barrique cellar, San Michele Appiano winery

Ausführung/Construction: 2005–2006
Bauherrschaft/Client: Kellerei St. Michael Eppan
Architektur/Architecture: Walter Angonese
Mitarbeiter/Collaborators: Silvia Boday, Katrin Lahner
Bauingenieur / Structural engineer: Armin Lahner
Künstlerische Intervention / Artistic intervention: Manfred Alois Mayr

Die Kellerei St. Michael Eppan ist eine erfolgreiche Winzergenossenschaft, die sich im Gegensatz zu ihren Mitbewerbern für keine grosse Lösung, sondern für kleinere bauliche Interventionen entschied. Einer dieser Umbauten erfolgte in den beiden Barriquekellern im historischen Kellergebäude aus dem Jahre 1906. Durch einen massiven Umbau des ehemaligen Lagerkellers, unter dem die Harmonie des Raumes litt, waren die Voraussetzungen für eine neue Nutzung dieses repräsentativen Raumes sehr schwierig. Gerade diese Sachzwänge wurden nun allerdings zur Grundlage des Entwurfs. Das Ergebnis ist ein an einen gewölbten Raum erinnernder, jedoch rechteckiger neuer Schaukeller, der die massiven statischen Elemente über Flächen zusammenfasst und dadurch eine neue Raumstimmung generiert. Der Putz aus über 20 000 verschiedenfarbigen zertrümmerten Weinflaschen lässt eine einzigartige Stimmung entstehen. Durch die neu geschaffene Begehbarkeit der ehemaligen Weinzisternen und den Rückbau des durch Umbauten in Mitleidenschaft gezogenen historischen Gewölbekellers konnten zwei repräsentative Räume geschaffen werden.

The San Michele Appiano winery is a successful wine making cooperative that – unlike its competitors – prefers small building interventions rather than large solutions. One such conversion was carried out in both barrique cellars in the historical cellar building from 1906. A massive conversion of the former storage cellar, which negatively affected the harmony of the space, made the underlying conditions for a new type of use for this prestigious space very difficult. It was precisely those constraints, however, that formed the basis for the design. The result is an exhibition cellar that recalls a vaulted space, but is actually rectangular, grouping the massive load-bearing elements together over the area and thereby creating a new spatial atmosphere. The plaster made from over 20,000 differently coloured, crushed wine bottles creates a unique atmosphere. It is now possible to walk through the wine cistern area, while the historical vaulted cellar, which had been undermined by the earlier conversion, was dismantled to create two prestigious rooms.

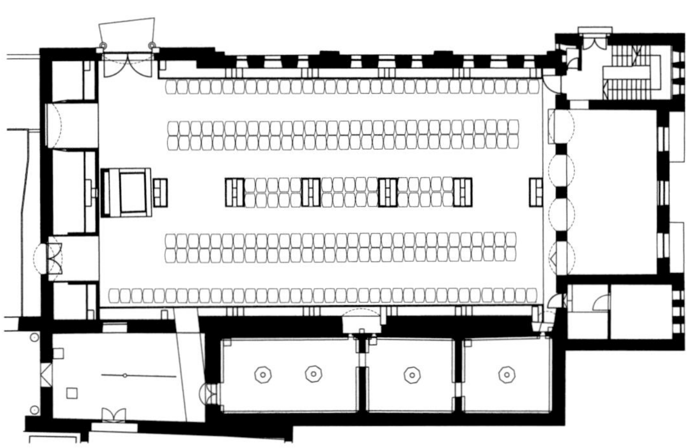

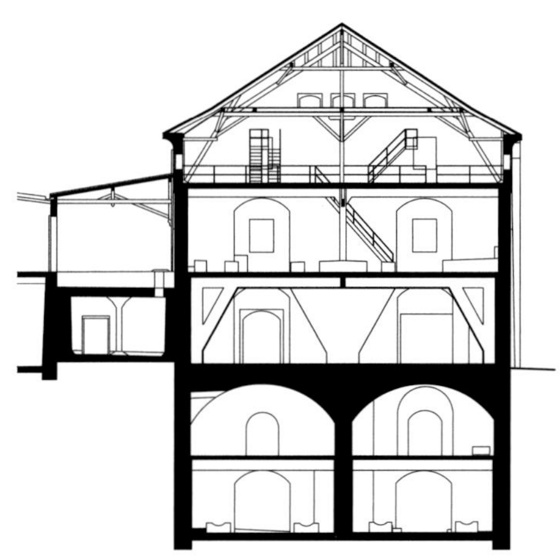

10 m

Wohnung R

Apartment R

Ausführung/Construction: 2007
Bauherrschaft/Client: privat/private
Architektur/Architecture:
Walter Angonese
Mitarbeiter/Collaborators:
Theo Gallmetzer, Katrin Lahner
Bauingenieur / Structural engineer:
Herbert Mair
Künstlerische Intervention / Artistic intervention: Manfred Alois Mayr

Das Dachgeschoss eines historischen Gehöfts in Girlan wurde vor über 20 Jahren ausgebaut. Dem neuen Nutzer entsprach dieser Umbau nicht, sodass eine massive Umgestaltung notwendig wurde. Neben einer Neueinteilung der Wohnfläche mit Bädern, Küche und zwei Schlafzimmern wurde eine «Schlafbrücke» implantiert, die die Raumhöhe ausnutzt, gleichzeitig aber leicht im Raum schwebt. Eine grosszügige Terrasse und ein neuer externer Treppenabgang in den Gartenbereich schaffen ansonsten bei Dachwohnungen selten vorhandene Freiräume.
Durch den Umbau konnte der Wohnung eine stärkere bürgerliche Identität verliehen werden, die besser zum Gesamterscheinungsbild des stattlichen Wohnhauses aus dem 19. Jahrhundert passt und auch deutlicher das Thema des Weiterbauens im Sinne Angoneses widerspiegelt. Gezielt eingesetzte und semantisch reflektierte Materialien wie Lehmputze, dunkles Eichenholz und hochglanzlackierte Oberflächen charakterisieren diese Baumassnahme, die wie in vielen Projekten dieses Architekten auch bewusst gesetzte Brüche nicht verleugnet.

The loft of a historical farmstead in Cornaiano was extended over 20 years ago. The conversion was not suitable for the new user, making a massive redesign necessary. In addition to a new division of the living space, with baths, a kitchen and two bedrooms, a "sleeping bridge" was implanted that uses the room's height, but also hovers slightly in the room. A large terrace and a new external staircase descending to the garden create open spaces that are otherwise rare in loft apartments.
The conversion gave the apartment a stronger bourgeois identity that suits the overall appearance of the stately 19th century house and also highlights Angonese's theme of "keep on building". The targeted use of semantically reflected materials such as loam rendering, dark oak wood and highly polished, varnished surfaces characterise the building measure, which, like many of his projects, does not deny its deliberately placed breaks.

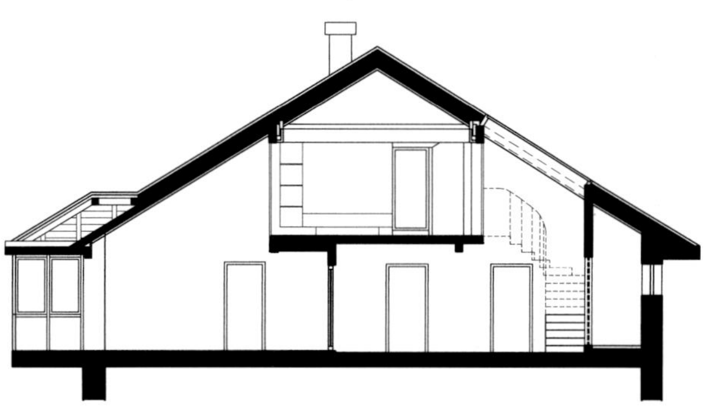

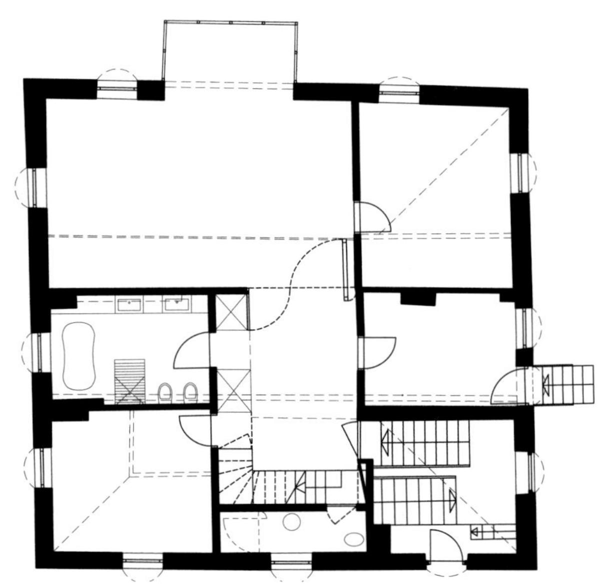

5 m

Bar ett?

ett? bar

Ausführung/Construction:
2006–2007
Bauherrschaft/Client:
Hildegard Stabinger
Architektur/Architecture:
Walter Angonese
Mitarbeiter/Collaborator:
Theo Gallmetzer
Künstlerische Intervention / Artistic intervention: Manfred Alois Mayr

Das ehemals bekannte Hotel Post in Bruneck wurde abgebrochen und durch einen schlichten Neubau ersetzt. Im Erdgeschoss wurde neben weiteren gastronomischen Betrieben und Geschäften eine kleine und schmale Bar untergebracht. Die Enge des Raumes, die geringe Raumhöhe und die Auseinandersetzung im Entwurfsprozess mit dem Phänomen Erinnerung haben zu einer auf das Thema Komfort fokussierten Lösung geführt. Eine lange Theke, ein Balken der sein «Vorbild», die american bar von Loos, nicht verleugnet, eine Sitzbank mit verschiebbaren kleinen Tischen, spezielle Leuchten und haptische Materialien generieren eine besondere Stimmung.
So wurden dunkles Eichenholz, Spiegelelemente, rauer Spritzputz, Hochglanzedelstahlrahmen und grauer Sandstein so ambivalent eingesetzt, dass der Bar eine gewisse Zeitlosigkeit anhaftet, was auch planerische Absicht war und zur Entwurfsmethodik Angoneses gehört.

The formerly renowned Hotel Post in Brunico was demolished and replaced by a simple new building. On the ground floor, a small, narrow bar was accommodated in addition to other catering services and shops. The tight space, the low room height and a study on the phenomenon of remembrance during the design process led to a solution that focuses on the theme of comfort. A long bar, a beam that does not deny being inspired by the Loos American Bar, a bench with small, moveable tables, special lights and haptic materials all create a special atmosphere.
Dark oak wood, mirror elements, coarse spray plaster, highly polished stainless steel frames and grey sandstone are implemented in such an ambivalent way that the bar gains a certain timelessness, which conforms with the planning intentions and is part of Angonese's design methods.

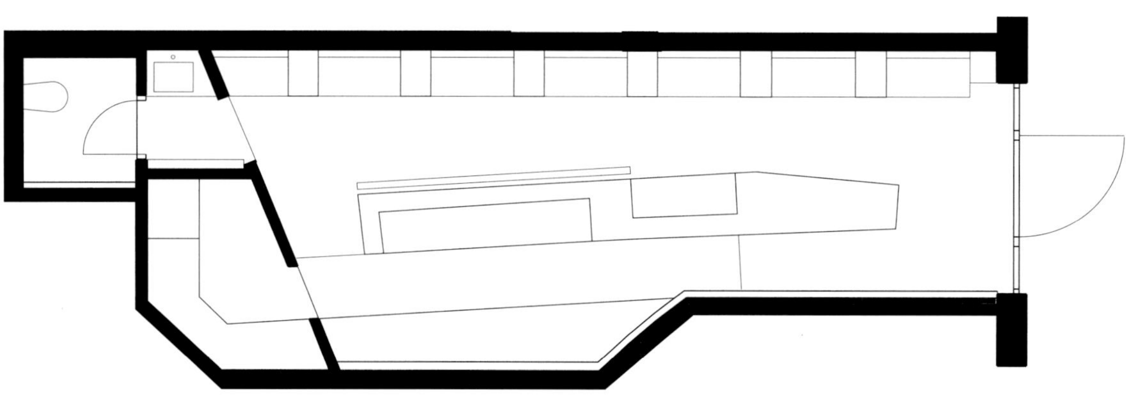

ett?
William Shakespeare
HAMLET

Eingangspavillon Gretl am See

Gretl am See entrance pavilion

Ausführung/Construction: 2005–2008
Bauherrschaft/Client: Klaus Maran
Architektur/Architecture: Walter Angonese
Mitarbeiter/Collaborators: Theo Gallmetzer, Thomas Tschöll
Bauingenieur / Structural engineers: Stahlbau Pichler
Künstlerische Intervention / Artistic intervention: Manfred Alois Mayr

Das Seebad Gretl am See wurde 1972 von Othmar Barth errichtet. Der Eingang führte über eine *promenade d'architecture* vom Parkplatz zum Seebad und zum Restaurant. Ein neues Verkehrskonzept relativierte 2007 die Logik der Erschliessung, was eine Art Torbau zum Seebad vonnöten machte. Der Eingangspavillon markiert den Startpunkt des Barth'schen Parcours, beherbergt einen kleinen Kiosk mit Bar und Sitzgelegenheiten, der – da an der Seepromenade gelegen – eine hohe Kundenfrequenz aufweist. Gänzlich in Stahl ausgeführt, leitet das Objekt die ankommenden Autofahrer direkt auf den Parkplatz, während entlang der Seepromenade ein weit ausladendes Vordach die Gäste empfängt. Eine lange Sitzbank mit Vitrine schliesst den Vorbereich zum Parkplatz hin ab. Der Kiosk ist so konzipiert, dass er für unterschiedliche Veranstaltungen flexibel nutzbar ist.

The Gretl am See lido was built in 1972 by Othmar Barth. The entrance led along the *promenade d'architecture* from the car park to the beach and restaurant. In 2007, a new transport concept changed the logic of that access situation, making a kind of gate structure necessary for the lido. The entrance pavilion marks the start of the Barth grounds and accommodates a small kiosk and bar with seating – which is highly frequented due to its situation on the lakeside promenade. Made entirely out of steel, the building guides the arriving drivers directly to the car park, while along the lakeside promenade, a broad-projecting canopy receives the guests. A long bench with glass showcases concludes the front area towards the car park. The kiosk is conceived in a way to make it flexibly usable for different events.

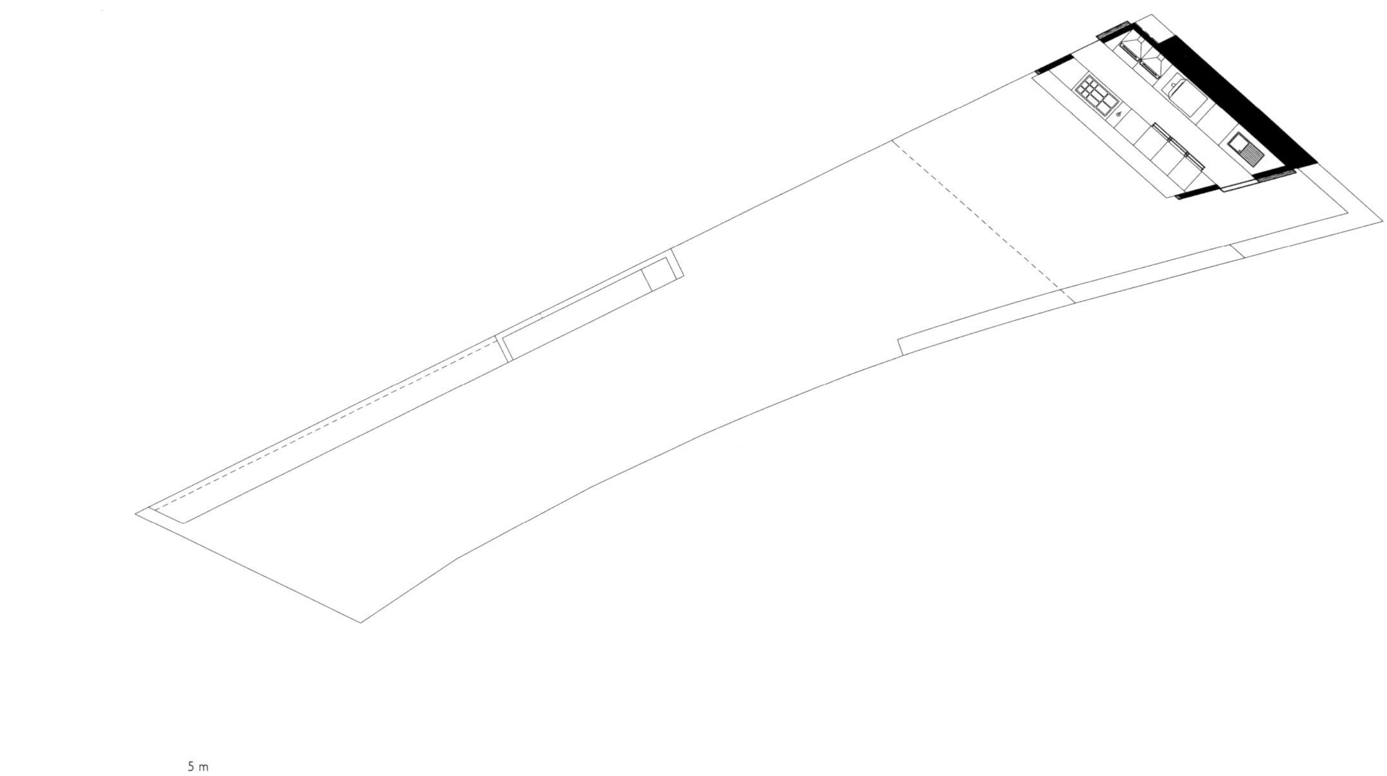

gretl am see
kiosk

Sparkasse Kaltern

Sparkasse Caldaro

Ausführung/Construction: 2006–2008
Bauherrschaft/Client: Sparim AG
Architektur/Architecture: Walter Angonese
Mitarbeiter/Collaborators: Theo Gallmetzer, Katrin Lahner, Thomas Tschöll
Bauingenieur / Structural engineers: Ingenieurteam Bergmeister
Landschaftsgestaltung / Landscape design: Roland Dellagiacoma
Künstlerische Intervention / Artistic intervention: Manfred Alois Mayr

Mehr als 30 Jahre nach dem letzten Umbau beschloss die Südtiroler Sparkasse, das gesamte Gebäude, in welchem sich auch mehrere Mietwohnungen befinden, einer Generalsanierung zu unterziehen. Der Bedarf an zusätzlichen Büro- und Schalterflächen konnte durch die Unterbauung eines mit Erde gefüllten Innenhofes erzielt werden. Der neue, mit begehbaren Glasflächen versehene Innenhof stellt weiterhin den Hauptzugang zu den Wohnbereichen dar, dient aber auch als Veranstaltungsort und Zugang zur Sparkassengalerie, die für verschiedene Kulturveranstaltungen neu konzipiert wurde. Durch die Verlegung der Schalterhalle aus den dunklen Räumlichkeiten des Renaissancebaus konnten ein grosszügiger Servicebereich und weitere Büroräumlichkeiten mit Blick auf einen kleinen Landschaftsgarten realisiert werden. Alle Wohnungen wurden generalsaniert, wobei der bürgerliche Wohnkomfort, den diese einst hatten, durch den Einsatz von edlen Materialien und Architekturdetails zeitgenössisch interpretiert wurde.

More than 30 years after its last conversion, the Südtiroler Sparkasse building society decided to completely renovate the building, which includes several rented apartments. The need for more offices and counters was fulfilled by underpinning an interior courtyard previously filled with earth. The new inner courtyard, with walkable glass areas, is still used as the main access to the apartments, but also as an event venue and provides access to the Sparkasse gallery, which was newly conceived for various cultural events. By moving the counter hall out of the dark rooms of the renaissance building, it was possible to create a spacious service area and other offices with views of a small landscape garden. All apartments were completely overhauled, whereby the comfortable bourgeois living quality they once had was reinterpreted in a contemporary way using elegant materials and architectural details.

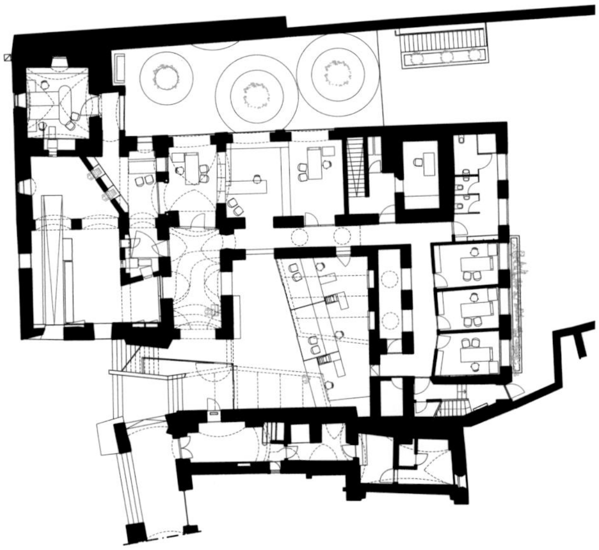

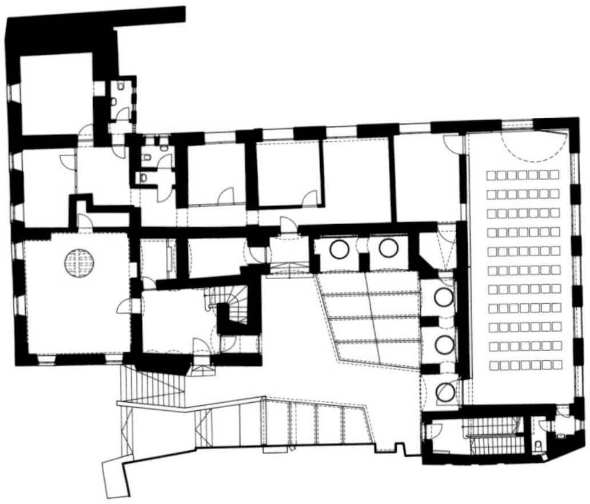

10 m

Ausführung/Construction:
2006–2009
Bauherrschaft/Client: Forst- und Domänenverwaltung Südtirol
Architektur/Architecture:
Walter Angonese
Mitarbeiter/Collaborators:
Theo Gallmetzer, Manfred Rauch
Bauingenieur / Structural engineer:
Herbert Mair
Künstlerische Intervention / Artistic intervention: Manuela Kerer, Manfred Alois Mayr
Kurator/Curator: Petra Paolazzi

Besucherzentrum Karersee

Der Karersee ist eines der Highlights des Weltnaturerbes Dolomiten. Jährlich wird er von mehr als einer Million Besuchern frequentiert, was eine Vielzahl von Souvenir- und Gastronomieständen entstehen liess. Diesem Wildwuchs wollten die Verantwortlichen Einhalt gebieten, gleichzeitig sollte ein barrierefreier Zugang zum See geschaffen werden. Der neue Weg führt vom Parkplatz über eine schräge, überdachte Rampe zu einer ehemaligen Unterführung aus dem Jahre 1888, um dann in den Seerundweg überzugehen. An diesen Rampenkörper schliessen im Erdgeschoss Verkaufs- und Gastronomieräume an, während hangseitig eine Stützmauer einen kleinen Innenhof für den Aufenthalt der Besucher schafft. Da sich in unmittelbarer Nähe ein Sägewerk befindet, wurde mit Holz aus der Region ein ca. 70 Meter langes und 4,5 Meter hohes Gebäude errichtet. Das Brett ist Grundmodul der gesamten Gestaltung, auch der in Beton ausgeführten Räume. Ein Ausstellungskonzept zur Geschichte des Ortes und mehrere künstlerische Interventionen ergänzen das Projekt.

Lake of Carezza visitor centre

The Lake of Carezza is one of the highlights of the World Cultural Heritage of the Dolomites. Every year more than a million people visit it, resulting in a large number of souvenir shops and food kiosks. The authorities aimed to control this unhindered development, while also providing barrier-free access to the lake. The new path leads from the car park along a sloping, covered ramp to a former underpass built in 1888, before ending at the circular route around the lake. Ground-floor sales and catering spaces are connected to the ramp structure, while on the slope side, a supporting wall creates a small interior courtyard for visitors to linger. Since a sawmill is located in the direct vicinity, timber from the region was used to build an approximately 70 metre long and 4.5 metre high building. Boards serve as the basic module of the entire design, including the rooms that are made of concrete. An exhibition concept to present the history of the location and several artistic interventions complement the project.

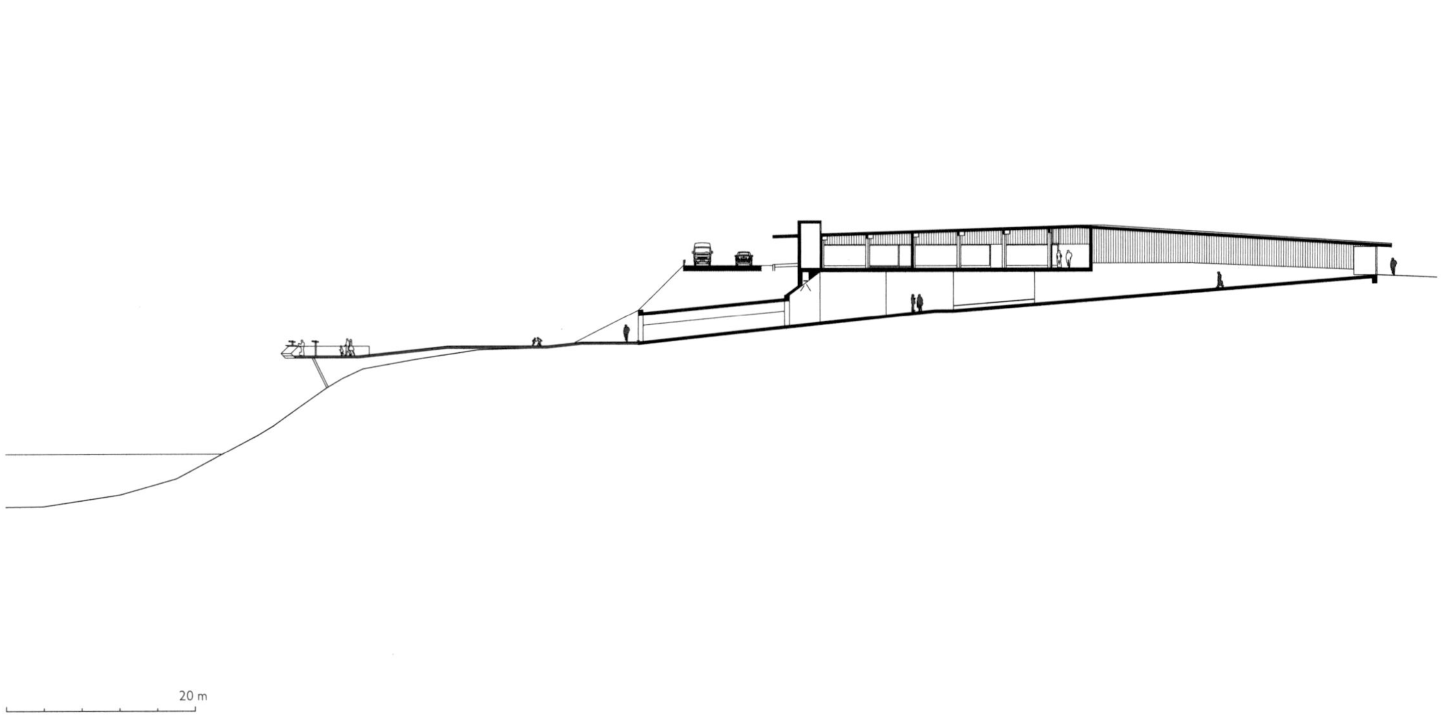

zum SEE / al LAGO
zum SEE / al LAGO

Umbau und Erweiterung der Grundschule Neumarkt

Conversion and extension of the Egna primary school

Ausführung/Construction: 2009–2010
Bauherrschaft/Client: Marktgemeinde Neumarkt
Architektur/Architecture: Walter Angonese
Mitarbeiter/Collaborators: Katrin Lahner, Thomas Tschöll, Lukas Wielander
Bauingenieur / Structural engineer: Hansjörg Letzner
Künstlerische Intervention / Artistic intervention: Manfred Alois Mayr

Die Grundschule Neumarkt wurde 1908 von Wilhelm Anton Linke im Münchner Jugendstil errichtet und in den frühen 1990er Jahren erstmals umgebaut, was dem Schulbau eine funktionalistische Erscheinung verlieh. Neben der Restaurierung waren neue Klassenräume, ein Werkraum und eine Bibliothek gefordert. Für die Bibliothek konnte der nicht mehr benötigte Turnsaal genutzt werden, während gegen Nordosten ein neues Volumen angebaut wurde, in welchem jeweils zwei Klassen mit Nebenräumen und Garderoben beziehungsweise der Werkraum und eine öffentliche Dachterrasse untergebracht wurden. Der mit Silikatfaserplatten gedämmte Neubau erhielt eine Putzoberfläche, die sich von ihrer Handwerklichkeit an der Oberfläche des Jugendstilgebäudes orientiert, jedoch über die Massstabsverfremdung (Kammputz mit 10 Zentimeter Wellenradius) ambivalent wirkt. Ein niedriges Eingangsgebäude dient als Verbindung zwischen den neuen Volumina und dem Altbau. Seine Proportionen orientieren sich an der Grösse der Kinder und bewegen sich am unteren Limit der rechtlich zulässigen Norm.

The Egna primary school was built in a Munich art nouveau style by Wilhelm Anton Linke in 1908 and converted for the first time in the early 1990s, giving the school building a functionalist appearance. In addition to the restoration, new classrooms, a workshop and a library were required. The no longer used gymnasium was used for the library, while towards the northeast, a new structure was built to accommodate two classes including auxiliary rooms and cloakrooms, plus a workshop and a public rooftop terrace. The new building, which is insulated with silicate fibre boards, received a plastered surface that is orientated towards the surface of the art nouveau building in terms of its craftsmanship, but given an ambivalent expression due to its alien scale (comb plaster with a 10-centimetre wave-radius). A low entrance building serves to connect the new volume to the old building. Its proportions are orientated towards the size of the children and are at the lowest legally permissible limit.

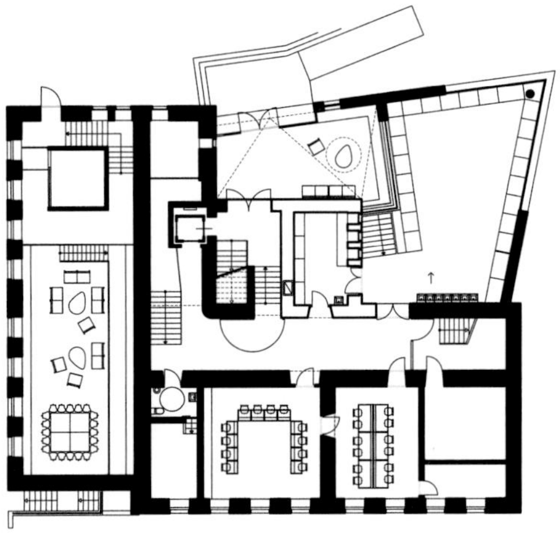

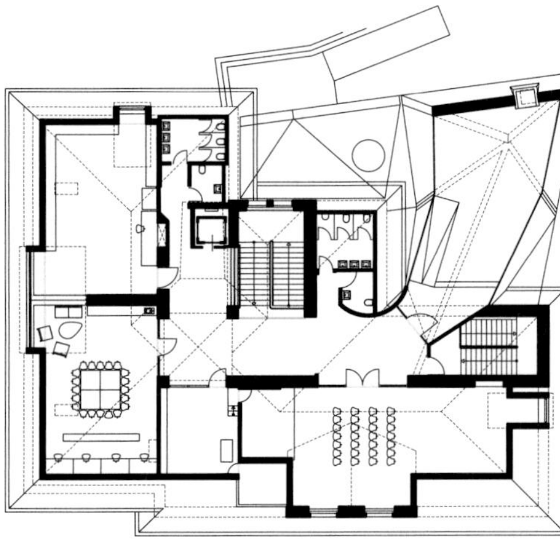

10 m

Vinothek der Kellerei St. Michael Eppan

Wine shop, San Michele Appiano winery

Ausführung/Construction: 2009–2010
Bauherrschaft/Client: Kellerei St. Michael Eppan
Architektur/Architecture: Walter Angonese
Mitarbeiter/Collaborator: Silvia Potente
Bauingenieur / Structural engineer: Armin Lahner
Künstlerische Intervention / Artistic intervention: Manfred Alois Mayr
Kurator/Curator: Petra Paolazzi
Grafisches Konzept/Graphics: Kurt Höretzeder, Daniele Lupo, Angelika Purtscher

Der Umbau der Vinothek der Kellerei St. Michael Eppan reagiert auf den Trend neuer Vinotheken, die oft zwar viel Design, aber nur wenig Wein zeigen. In diesem Fall versteht sich die Architektur als Hintergrund, die die Vielfalt des Weinsortiments zelebriert, Aufenthaltsqualität schafft und mit einem didaktischen Objekt mit dem Titel «Alles über Wein» das Wesentliche in den Mittelpunkt des Konzepts stellt. Materialien wie massive Eiche, Bitu-Terrazzo und Glas bestimmen die Atmosphäre, Licht wird szenografisch verwendet. Die Zusammenarbeit mit dem Künstler Manfred Alois Mayr lässt die Grenzen zwischen künstlerischer Intervention und Architektur verschmelzen. Mit der neuen Toreinfahrt, der 70 Meter langen Stahlpergola und der Verwebung der bereits in den späten 1990er Jahren errichteten Porphyrbetonwände, die 2014 eine Vollendung mit einem nordseitig gelegenen Themengarten erhalten haben, sind die punktuellen Interventionen für die über 100-jährige Weinkellerei St. Michael Eppan über einen längeren Zeitraum vorerst abgeschlossen.

The conversion of the wine shop for the San Michele Appiano winery reacts to the trend of new wine houses, which often have a great deal of design, but do not present much wine. In this case, the architecture regards itself as a background that celebrates the diversity of the wine on offer, creating a quality atmosphere for people to linger. It also uses an educational area entitled "All about wine" to focus on the most important theme of the concept. Materials such as solid oak, Bitu-Terrazzo and glass determine the atmosphere, while lighting is used scenographically. The co-operation with the artist Manfred Alois Mayr merged the boundaries between artistic intervention and architecture. With the new gate entrance, the 70 metre long steel pergola and the interlocking porphyry concrete wall from the late 1990s, which were completed in 2014 with a theme garden to the north, concludes for the foreseeable future the selective interventions to the 100-year-old San Michele Appiano winery, which were undertaken over a long period.

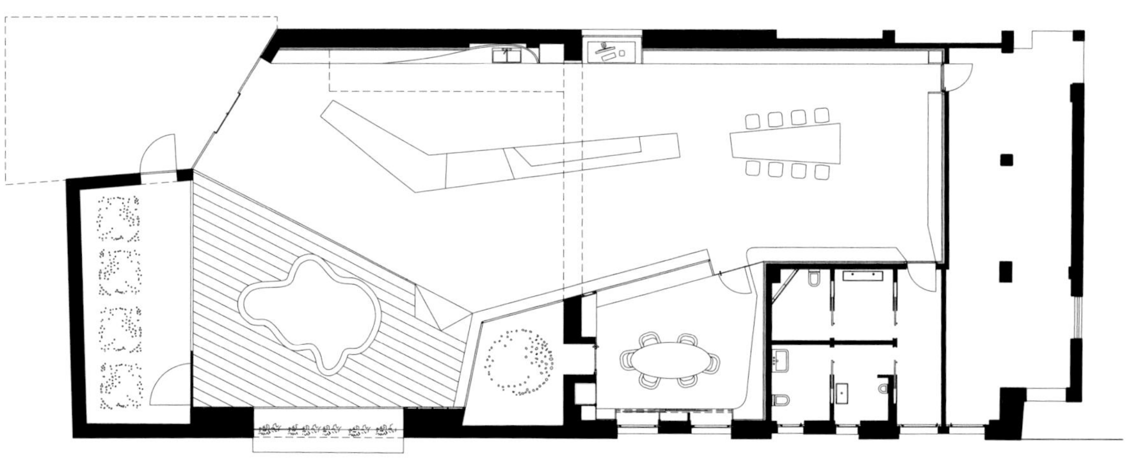

5 m

Ausführung/Construction: 2007–2011
Bauherrschaft/Client: privat/private
Architektur/Architecture: Walter Angonese
Mitarbeiter/Collaborators: Katrin Lahner, Silvia Potente, Thomas Tschöll
Bauingenieur / Structural engineer: Hansjörg Letzner
Landschaftsgestaltung / Landscape design: Freilich Landschafts-architektur

Haus V

In den Weinbergen oberhalb von Kaltern gelegen und geplant für eine vierköpfige Familie, mit Garten und Schwimmbad, nimmt der Entwurf Formen und Materialien der Umgebung und der Bautradition auf und interpretiert sie neu: ein Experiment mit Brüchen, die Ambivalenz zu erzeugen versuchen. Charakteristisch ist die Vielzahl von Loggien und Patios, eine Referenz an die Überetscher Bautradition, die dem Haus ein gewisses Volumen verleihen und es semantisch mehr zu einem landwirtschaftlichen Hof in den Weinbergen als zu einem Wohngebäude machen soll. Das Gebäude wurde von innen nach aussen entworfen, um die spektakulären Ausblicke räumlich fassen zu können. Es entstand ein Haus, das die sehr restriktiven gesetzlichen Vorgaben des Bauens in Südtirol im Sinne der Diktion «von der Norm zur Form» auf eigene Weise interpretiert.

House V

Situated in the vineyards above Caldaro and planned for a family of four, including a garden and swimming pool, the design picks up on forms and materials of the surrounding landscape and building tradition, yet reinterprets them: the experiment with breaks aims to create ambivalence. The large number of loggias and patios is typical, a reference to the building tradition of the Überetsch region, aimed at giving the building a certain volume and making the house semantically more an agricultural farm in the vineyards than a residential building. It was designed from the inside out in order to spatially frame the spectacular views. The result is a house that interprets the highly restrictive building regulations in South Tyrol in the sense of developing "the form out of the norm" in an autonomous way.

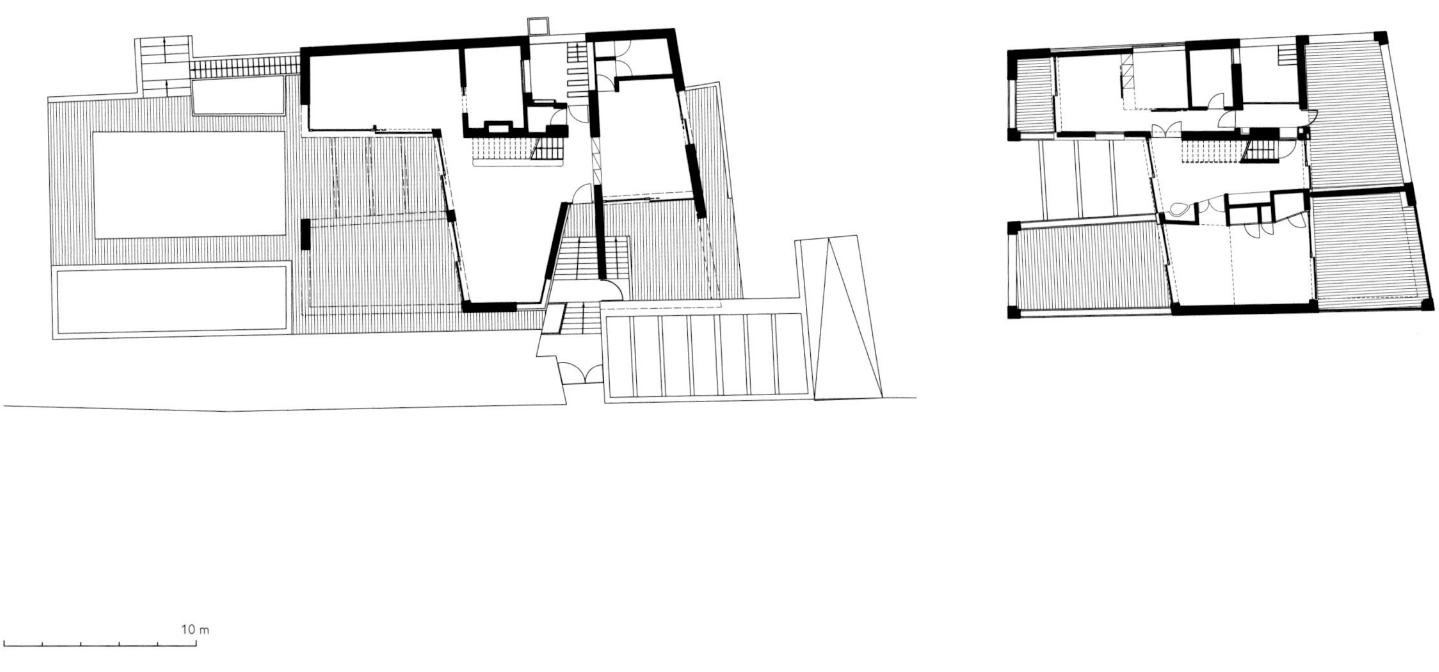

Sammlerhaus D

Ausführung/Construction: 2006–2011
Bauherrschaft/Client: privat/private
Architektur/Architecture: Walter Angonese, Andrea Marastoni
Mitarbeiter/Collaborators: Alessia Bergamo, Christoph Gapp, Matthias Mayr, Silvia Potente, Giorgio Larcher, Thomas Tschöll
Bauingenieur / Structural engineer: Stefano Mattei
Landschaftsgestaltung / Landscape design: Freilich Landschaftsarchitektur
Künstlerische Intervention / Artistic intervention: Robert Barry, Antony Gormley, Dan Graham

Der Wunsch eines Kunstsammlers, ein Haus zu planen, in welchem er mit seiner Sammlung leben kann, war die Vorgabe. Entgegen anderen Beispielen, wo das Wohnen vom Sammeln getrennt ist, wurde in diesem Fall ein Konzept entwickelt, wo sich das Wohnen in die Galerieräume ausdehnen und die Sammlung bis in die privaten Bereiche vordringen kann. Der Anspruch nach formaler Neutralität wurde zugunsten einer räumlichen Komplexität aufgegeben. Alle Räume des fünfgeschossigen Gebäudes, das in den steilen Hang gesetzt ist, sind aufgrund ihrer Lage und der gezielt gesetzten Öffnungen zum Aussenraum unterschiedlich. Hohen Räumen folgen niedrige, funktionelle Bereiche sind dazwischen eingespannt, um im fünften Geschoss in einem Wohn- und Kunstraum zu enden. Ein sägerauer Eichenboden wie in Werkstätten durchzieht alle Räume. Diffuses Kunstlicht wird überall, auch in den Wohnbereichen, eingesetzt. Das Aushubmaterial (Porphyr) diente als Zuschlag für den Beton der aufgeraut wurde, die Textur der umgebenden Felsen aufnimmt und damit den topografischen Ansatz des Projekts unterstreicht.

Collector's house D

An art collector wished to plan a house in which he could live with his collection. Unlike other examples, where the living and collection areas are separate, this design developed a concept where the living areas extend into the gallery rooms and the collection can extend into the private areas. The demand for formal neutrality was dropped in favour of a spatial complexity. All rooms of the five-storey building, which is situated on a steep slope, are different as a result of their position and the targeted placement of the openings towards the exterior space. Tall rooms are followed by low, functional areas inserted in between, ending on the fifth floor with a living and art room. A rough-sawn oak floor, like those used in workshops, covers all the rooms. Diffuse artificial light is used everywhere, even in the living areas. The excavated material (porphyry) is used as an aggregate for the concrete, which was roughened, thereby assuming the texture of the surrounding cliffs and highlighting the topographical approach of the project.

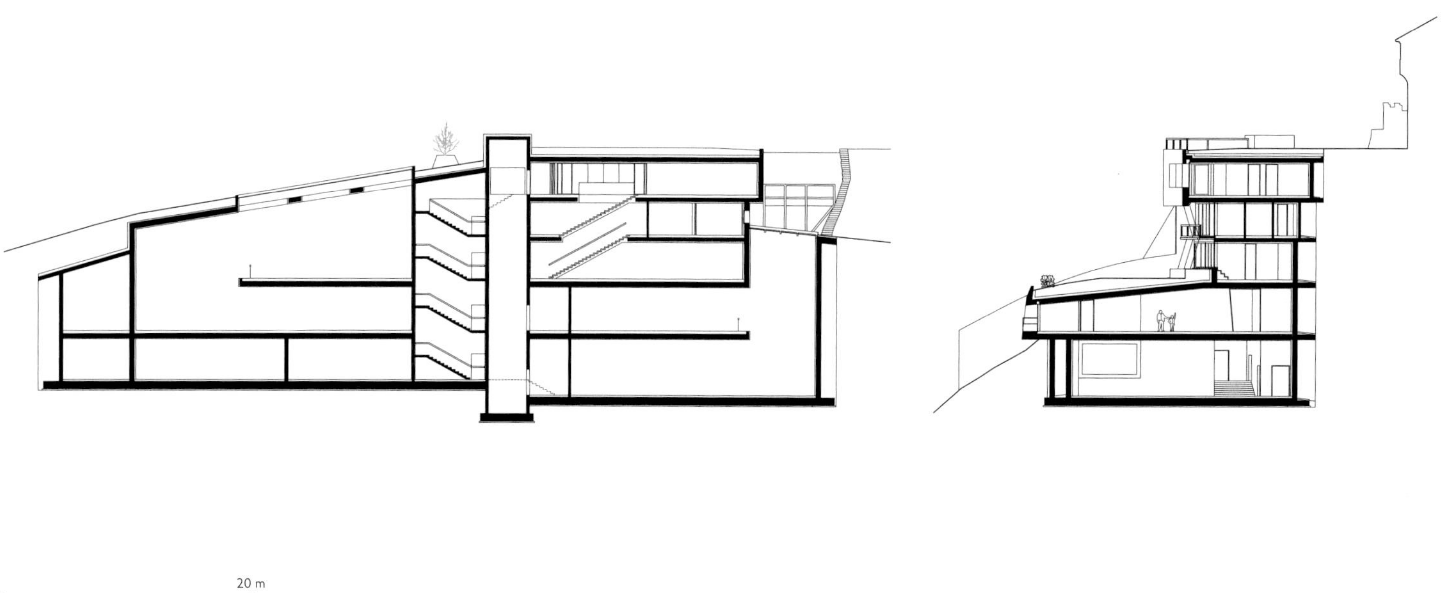

Haus T

Ausführung/Construction: 2010–2013
Bauherrschaft/Client: privat/private
Architektur/Architecture: Walter Angonese
Mitarbeiter/Collaborator: Martin Trebo
Bauingenieur / Structural engineers: Ingenieurteam Bergmeister

Haus T war eine klassische Aufgabe, nämlich das Erweitern eines Bestands mit generationsübergreifendem Anspruch. Das Ausreizen der gesetzlichen Vorgaben in Bezug auf Höhe und neue Kubatur, das erst durch die energetische Sanierung des Bestands möglich wurde, führte zum Ansatz des einfachen Weiterbauens, das aber mit zahlreichen Brüchen eine gewisse Ambivalenz beansprucht. Das Konzept, den Zubau gegenüber dem eingeschossigen Altbau in die Höhe zu bringen und damit eine schöne Aussicht auf die Berggipfel der Dolomiten ermöglichen zu können, führte in Kombination mit dem gestalterischen Anspruch an einen aufgeständerten Wohnflügel, der aus rechtlichen Gründen mit dem Bestand zusammengebaut werden musste, zu einer neuen Dachform, die aus dem Walmdach des in den späten 1960er Jahren errichteten Hauses herauswächst. Das neue Dach nimmt die Materialität des bestehenden Daches auf und differenziert sich nur durch einen anderen figurativen und räumlichen Ansatz.

House T

Haus T was a classic task, namely to extend an existing building to accommodate multi-generation living. Exploiting the legal limits to the full with respect to the height and cubature, which only became possible through the energy-related renovation of the existing building, led to the approach of simple extension, though with many breaks to add a certain ambivalence. The concept of heightening the extension compared to the older building, thereby enabling a beautiful view of the peaks of the Dolomites, was combined with the design's demand for an elevated residential wing, which for legal reasons had to be built together with the existing structure, leading to a new roof form that grows out of the hip roof of the late 1960s building. The new roof picks up on the materials of the existing roof and only distinguishes itself through its different figurative and spatial approach.

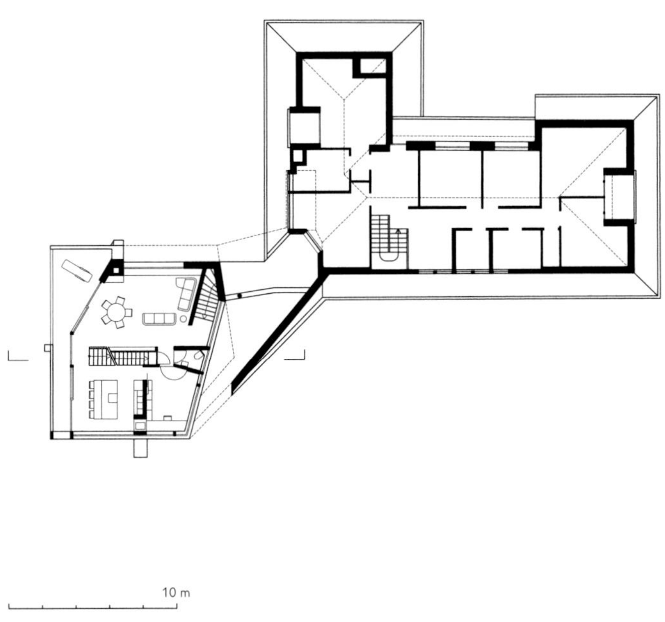

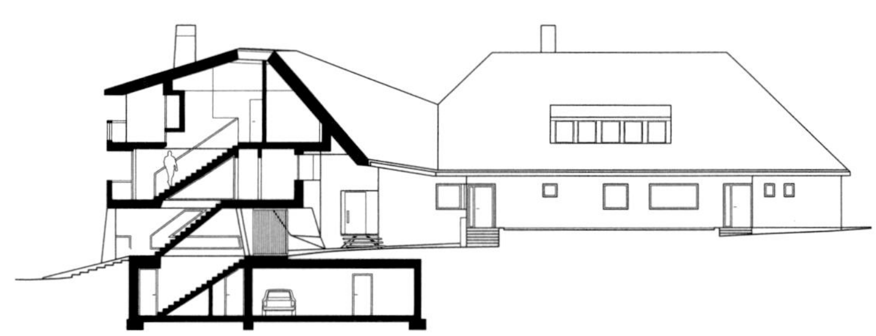

Feldhütte im Weinberg

Vineyard hut

Ausführung/Construction: 2014–2015
Bauherrschaft/Client: privat/private
Architektur/Architecture: Walter Angonese
Mitarbeiter/Collaborator: Kathrin Hofer
Bauingenieur / Structural engineer: Hansjörg Letzner
Künstlerische Intervention / Artistic intervention: Manfred Alois Mayr

Kaltern ist von zusammenhängenden Weinbergen umgeben, die allesamt unter Schutz stehen. Feldhütten – wie sie genannt werden – waren charakteristisch für diesen Landschaftsraum, sind aber aufgrund der Technisierung der Landwirtschaft in Vergessenheit geraten. Viele sind zerfallen, andere werden kaum mehr genutzt. Meist waren es kleine Holzbauten, manchmal auch gemauert, wo Arbeitsgeräte eingestellt wurden und man sich bei einer Marende mit Wein von den Strapazen des Alltags erholen konnte. Diese Tradition wollte der Bauherr wieder aufgreifen und eine kleine «Feldhütte» mit wunderbarem Blick auf den Kalterer See errichten. In Zusammenarbeit mit dem Künstler Manfred Alois Mayr wurden tradierte Typologien neu – durchaus auch ironisch angehaucht – interpretiert. Die gesetzlich maximal zulässige Grösse von 15 Quadratmetern wurde mit einigen Kunstgriffen ausgereizt: ein ausfahrbares Dach und auffaltbare Wände, die Innen- und Aussenraum trennen und eine Nutzung als Geräteschuppen ermöglichen, aber auch eine lukullische Stärkung erlauben.

Caldaro is surrounded by connected vineyards that are all preservation-listed. Vineyard huts – known as "Feldhütten" – were characteristic of this landscape, but have become forgotten due to technological advances in agriculture. Many are dilapidated, while others are hardly used. They were mostly small wooden buildings, sometimes in stone, where working tools were stored and one could recover from the daily work with a local "Marende" snack and a glass of wine. The client wished to revive that tradition and build a small "Feldhütte" with a wonderful view of Lake of Carezza. Together with the artist Manfred Alois Mayr, traditional typologies were reinterpreted – also with a hint of irony. The maximum legal size of 15 square metres was exploited to the full using a few tricks: a sliding roof and foldable walls separating the interior and exterior space allow its use both as a tool shed and as a place for Epicurean refreshment.

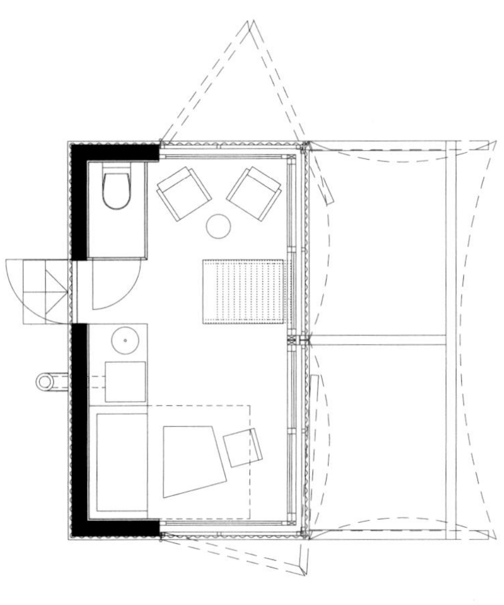

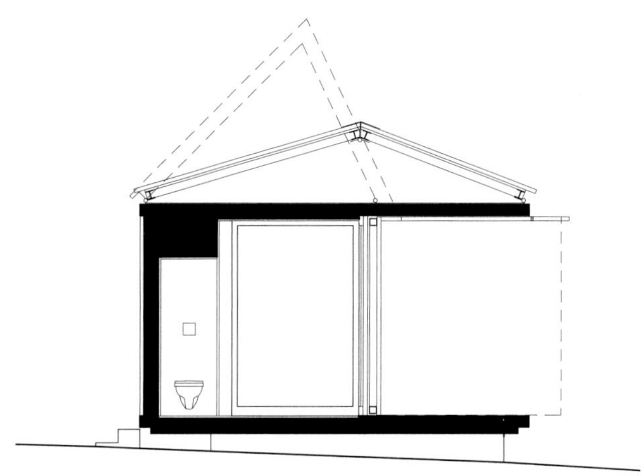

2.5 m

Tor und Gewächshaus, Ansitz Drescher

Gate and greenhouse, Drescher manor house

Ausführung/Construction: 2008–2009; 2015
Bauherrschaft/Client: Theo Drescher
Architektur/Architecture: Walter Angonese
Mitarbeiter/Collaborator: Jacopo Vantini

Der Ansitz «Reich am Platz» der Familie Drescher ist nicht nur der älteste Buschenschank Südtirols, sondern auch das wohl beste Beispiel und beliebtes Fotomotiv des sogenannten Überetscher Stils, einer Renaissancearchitektur, die im späten 16. und im 17. Jahrhundert verbreitet war. Der Ansitz besteht aus dem Haupthaus und einem grossen Wirtschaftsgebäude, die von einer historischen Mauer umfriedet sind. Entlang dieser Mauer wurde vor Jahren von Walter Angonese ein Gewächshaus für die Überwinterung der Pflanzen realisiert. Aus der verputzten Mauer wächst ein nach Süden und Westen verglaster Zweckbau, der über eine 4 Meter hohe Tür erschlossen wird. Pragmatische Überlegungen – das Regenwasser wird in einem aus dem Gebäude herauswachsenden Wasserbehälter gesammelt – und die Materialisierung charakterisieren das kleine Gebäude. In einem zweiten Schritt war die Errichtung eines neuen Tors für landwirtschaftliche Fahrzeuge erforderlich. Die Lösung ist, einen Teil der Mauer zu öffnen, ohne die schöne Umfriedung optisch zu beeinträchtigen.

The manor house "Reich am Platz" belonging to the Drescher family is not only the oldest "Buschenschank" tavern in South Tyrol, but also probably the best example of the popular photo motif of the so-called Überetsch style, a form of renaissance architecture that was widespread in the 16th and 17th centuries. The manor house consists of a main house and a large service building surrounded by a historical wall. Years ago, Walter Angonese built a greenhouse along the wall for plants to survive the winter. Facing the south and west, a glazed functional building grows out of the plastered wall, and is accessed using a 4-metre tall door. Pragmatic considerations – the rainwater is collected in a container that grows out of the building – and the material characterise the small building. In a second step, it was necessary to build a new gate for agricultural vehicles. The solution was to open part of the wall without negatively affecting its beautiful appearance.

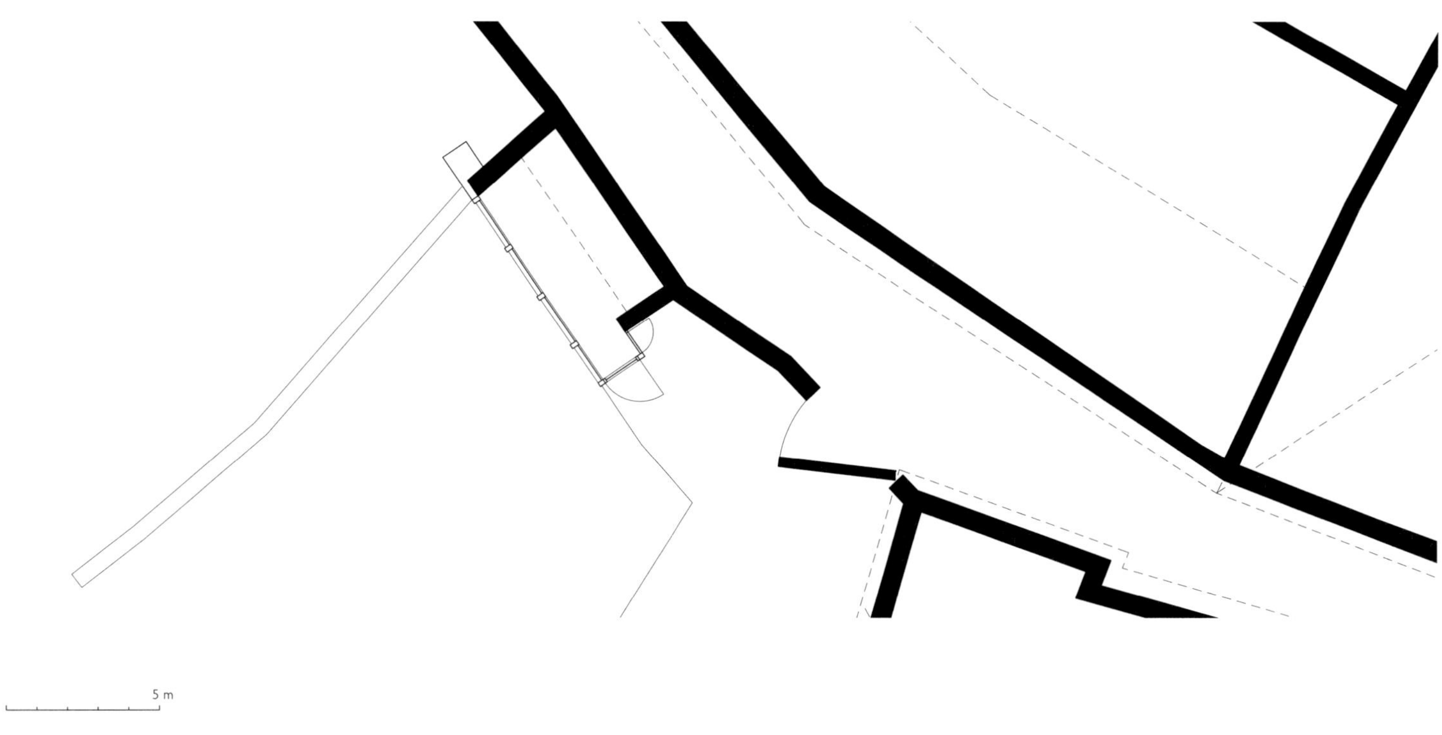

Weingut Thomas Pichler

Thomas Pichler winery

Ausführung/Construction:
2013–2016
Bauherrschaft/Client:
Thomas Pichler
Architektur/Architecture:
Walter Angonese
Mitarbeiter/Collaborators:
Martin Trebo, Thomas Tschöll,
Jacopo Vantini
Bauingenieur / Structural engineer:
Herbert Mair

Italien im Allgemeinen und Südtirol im Speziellen sind bekannt für viele gesetzliche Auflagen. Für ein sehr kleines Baufeld neben dem Heimathaus des Winzers sollte eine kleine Kellerei mit Lagerkeller und Verkostungsraum nebst Dienstwohnung errichtet werden. Abstände von den Grundstücksgrenzen und Höhenbeschränkungen konditionierten den Entwurfsprozess massgeblich. Schlussendlich wurden die normativen Vorgaben zum Entwurfsgenerator. Der skulpturale Charakter des oberirdischen Bauteils ist auf eine kreative Interpretation dieser normativen Vorgaben zurückzuführen. Ein sehr enges Budget verlangte nach einer maximalen Reduzierung des Materialaufwands, weshalb der Ortbeton (ohne Anspruch auf Sichtbeton) mit einer einfachen Schlemme versehen wurde. Die Verschiedenfarbigkeit ist gleichfalls auf unterschiedliche Farbansprüche seitens der Nachbarn und der Familie zurückzuführen und wurde ebenfalls als «Auflage» übernommen. Um die Dächer für eine Terrassenbenutzung freizuspielen, wurden die Solarkollektoren an die Fassade gehängt, was zusätzlich eine Beschattung der grossen Fensterflächen ermöglicht. Der Innenausbau ist gänzlich in Holz realisiert.

Italy in general and South Tyrol specifically are renowned for their many legal regulations. On a very small building site beside the home of the wine maker, a small cellar was planned including storage space and a tasting room beside the work apartment. The distances from the property boundaries and height restrictions defined the design process. The normative specifications ultimately became the design generator, as the sculptural character of the overground section of the building is based on a creative interpretation of those normative specifications. A very limited budget required the maximum reduction of materials, which is why the in-situ cast concrete (without fair-faced qualities) was treated with a simple coating. The different colours are also the result of different colour requirements with respect to the neighbours' and the family's wishes, which were also taken on board as a "condition". To free up the roofs for terrace use, solar panels were suspended on the façade, providing additional shade for the large window areas. The interior decoration is all in wood.

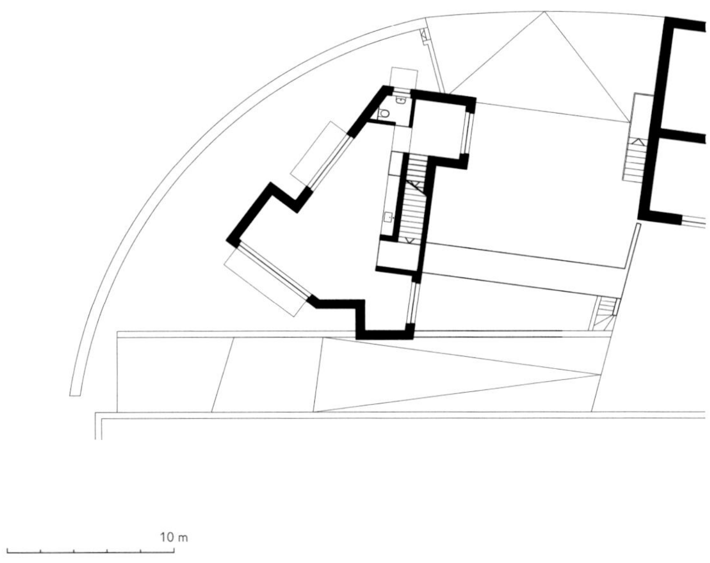

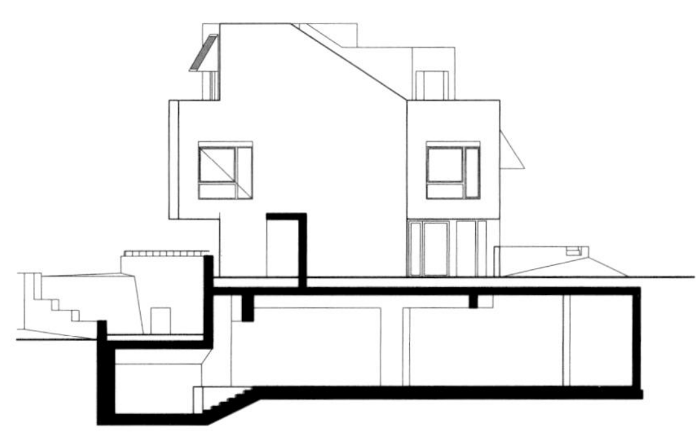

Wettbewerb/Competition: 2012
Bauherrschaft/Client: Autonome Provinz Bozen Südtirol
Architektur/Architecture: Walter Angonese
Mitarbeiter/Collaborators: Kathrin Hofer, Andrea Mazzucotelli, Martin Trebo, Thomas Tschöll
Bauingenieur / Structural engineer: Mario Monotti

Schwarzensteinhütte

Für eine der höchst gelegenen Schutzhütten der Ostalpen auf über 3000 Metern versucht der Entwurf, zwischen einem klassischen Schutzhaus und einer grossen, weit sichtbaren Biwakschachtel zu vermitteln. Gemeinsam mit dem Schweizer Ingenieur Mario Monotti wurde ein konstruktiv rational durchdachter Gerüstbau aus Holz konzipiert, der sich ohne Fundamente auf dem Fels über eine Mulde spannt und mit schweren Kupferplatten verkleidet werden sollte. Aus diesem Brückenbau wachsen warzenähnliche Fenster, die jede Schlafkoje mit Licht und Luft versehen, wobei am Dach der Gaupen eine Fotovoltaikplatte Energie für das Licht des jeweiligen Raums spendet. Aufgrund des extrem reduzierten Raumprogramms wäre dem durch die Konstruktion überdachten Aussenraum, der den Zugang zum Schutzhaus definiert, eine besondere Bedeutung zugekommen.

Schwarzenstein hut

The design for one of the highest altitude shelter huts in the eastern Alps, at over 3,000 metres, mediated between a classic shelter hut and a large, bivouac box that could be seen from afar. Together with the Swiss engineer Mario Monotti, the structurally rational scaffold building was conceived in wood, spanning over a hollow without any foundations in the cliff. Heavy copper plate cladding was planned. Wart-like windows grow out of the bridge construction, providing light and air for every bunk, whereby the roof of the dormers is equipped with a photovoltaic panel to provide energy for the light in each room. Due to the extremely reduced spatial programme, the covered exterior space defining the entrance to the shelter would have had a special significance.

Parkhaus Moena

Moena ist ein Touristenort im Fassatal, im Herzen der Dolomiten. Vor mehreren Jahren hat die Gemeinde ein neues Mobilitätskonzept erstellt, das verkehrsberuhigende Massnahmen und die Errichtung eines Parkhauses am Ortseingang vorsieht. Das Raumprogramm sah ein Gebäude für 280 Autos, eine Bar, eine Brücke zur Erschliessung des gegenüberliegenden Ortsteiles und die Neudefinition der Dorferschliessung mitsamt Kreisverkehr vor. Im zum Fluss hin stark abfallenden Gelände wurde ein sechsgeschossiges Parkhaus geplant, das die Autos in Wendungen bis auf Flusshöhe leitet und in eine Promenade ins historische Zentrum übergeht. Die Stellplätze wurden hangseitig vorgesehen, sodass die vorspringenden Erschliessungsrampen parallel zur Hangneigung eine neue Topografie schaffen und der etwa 25 Meter hohe Bau wie ein Schichtenmodell wirkt.

Moena car park

Moena is a tourist resort in the Fassa Valley, in the heart of the Dolomites. Several years ago, the community developed a new mobility concept involving traffic-calming measures and the construction of a multi-storey car park at the village entrance. The spatial programme intended a building for 280 cars, a bar, a bridge to provide access to the opposite side of the village and a redefinition of the village transport connections including a bypass. On the terrain, which is heavily inclined towards the river, a six-storey car park was planned that guides cars in a winding fashion down to the river level and merges with a promenade to the historical centre. The parking spaces were intended for the slope side, so that the protruding access ramps parallel to the slope create a new topography and the 25-metre high building had the effect of a layered model.

Wettbewerb/Competition: 2013
Architektur/Architecture: Walter Angonese, CN10 architetti (Gianluca Gelmini, Andrea Pressiani)
Beratung/Consultancy: Ingenieurteam Bergmeister

Neue Bibliothek Kaltern

New Caldaro library

Wettbewerb/Competition: 2013
Ausführung/Construction: 2016–
Bauherrschaft/Client:
Marktgemeinde Kaltern
Architektur/Architecture:
Walter Angonese
Mitarbeiter/Collaborators
(Wettbewerb/Competition):
Moritz Gaiser, Kathrin Hofer,
Andrea Mazzucotelli, Martin Trebo,
Thomas Tschöll
Mitarbeiter/Collaborators
(Ausführung/Construction):
Kathrin Schiefer, Martin Trebo,
Thomas Tschöll
Bauingenieur / Structural engineers:
Ingenieurteam Bergmeister
Künstlerische Intervention / Artistic
intervention: Manfred Alois Mayr

Kalterns derzeitige Bibliothek ist im Untergeschoss des Pfarrheimes untergebracht, was suboptimal ist und zum Konzept für ein neues «Haus des Wissens» führte. Es wurde ein geladener Wettbewerb ausgeschrieben und vom Büro Walter Angonese gewonnen. Das Gebäude wird am südlichen Ortsrand von Kaltern errichtet und ist durch ein grosses, bis zum Boden reichendes Dach charakterisiert, das nach einem Konzept von Manfred Alois Mayr mit Steingutfliesen verkleidet wird. Unter diesem Dach liegen auf vier Geschossen die rundum verglasten Räume der Bibliothek. Gezielt gesetzte Öffnungen im Dach gewährleisten nicht nur besondere Ausblicke auf die umgebende Landschaft, sondern beschatten durch ihre Gestaltung auch die Räume der Bibliothek. Im Entwurf werden vorhandene Elemente des Ortes zwar aufgegriffen, jedoch durch subtile Transformationen neu interpretiert. Neben den Kirchen, dem Gemeindeamt und der Schule soll die Bibliothek eindeutig als öffentliches, markantes Gebäude wahrgenommen werden und den turmartigen Abschluss des historischen Zentrums bilden.

The current library of Caldaro is accommodated in the basement of the rectory, which is not ideal and led to the development of a concept for a new "House of Knowledge". An invitation competition was announced and won by the office of Walter Angonese. The building will be constructed at the southern perimeter of the village and is characterised by a large roof that stretches down to the ground and will be clad in stoneware tiles according to a concept by Manfred Alois Mayr. The fully glazed rooms of the library are situated on four storeys. Precisely placed openings in the roof provide special views of the surrounding landscape and also shade for the library rooms due to their design. The design picks up on existing elements of the location, but these are reinterpreted through subtle transformations. Beside the churches, the municipal authorities and the school, the library should be clearly perceived as a public, striking building and form the tower-like conclusion of the historical centre.

Tinne Museum

Klausen war im späten 19. und frühen 20. Jahrhundert europaweit für seine Künstlerkolonie bekannt. Unter den Persönlichkeiten dieser Künstlerkolonie sticht der Maler Alexander Koester hervor. Um aber kein klassisches Sammlungsmuseum zu planen, wurde durch eine internationale Kuratorengruppe ein Kinder- und Familienmuseum konzipiert, in dem die Sammlung von Alexander Koester Teil eines museumsdidaktischen Konzepts mit Werkstätten und einem Museumscafé wird. Das gesamte ehemalige Kapuzinerkloster wird mit eingebunden.

Während zum Tinnebach hin eine massive «Mauer» die Gefährlichkeit des Bachs symbolisieren soll, fällt zur Klosteranlage ein steiles Betonpultdach zum Park ab. Ein in Form einer überdachten Brücke konzipierter offener Eingang verbindet das Museum mit der Altstadt von Klausen. Vom Eingang führt ein grosszügiger Treppenlauf zu den Werkstätten, Arbeitsräumen und dem Café auf der Parkebene, während ein anderer die permanente und die temporären Ausstellungshallen im Obergeschoss verbindet. Leicht eingefärbter Beton mit Zuschlägen des Tinnebachs und grossflächige Verglasungen prägen das Bauwerk.

Tinne Museum

In the late 19th and early 20th centuries, Chiusa was renowned throughout Europe for is artists' colony. Alexander Koester was an outstanding artist who lived there. To avoid planning a classic collection museum, an international group of curators designed a children's and family-friendly museum in which the collection of Alexander Koester becomes part of the museum's educational concept, including workshops and a museum café. The entire former Capuchin monastery is integrated.

While a massive "wall" faces the Tinnebach stream, symbolising its potential danger, a steep concrete pitched roof descends towards the monastery facility and the park. An open entrance conceived in the form of a covered bridge connects the museum to the old town of Chiusa. From the entrance, a spacious staircase leads to the workshops, workrooms and the café on the park level, while another connects the permanent and temporary exhibition halls on the upper floor. Slightly coloured concrete with aggregates from the Tinnebach stream and large-scale glazing characterise the building.

Studie/Study: 2016
Architektur/Architecture: Walter Angonese, Klaus Hellweger
Mitarbeiter/Collaborators: Karin Oberparleiter, Jacopo Vantini
Beratung/Consultancy: Ingenieurteam Bergmeister
Künstlerische Intervention / Artistic intervention: Manfred Alois Mayr
Kuratorenteam / Curator team: Carl Kraus, Petra Paolazzi, Marion Piffer Damiani

Landhaus D

Country house D

Wettbewerb/Competition: 2015
Ausführung/Construction: 2016–
Bauherrschaft/Client: privat/private
Architektur/Architecture:
Walter Angonese
Mitarbeiter/Collaborators:
Francesco Flaim, Quirin Prünster
Bauingenieur / Structural engineer:
Robert Kofler (Mader & Flatz)
Landschaftsgestaltung / Landscape
design: Maria Auböck, Janos Káráz

Als Siegerprojekt aus einem international geladenen Wettbewerb hervorgegangen, verbindet das Gebäude topografische und typologische Ansprüche. Die Einfügung dieses beträchtlichen Volumens – ein Ensemble aus eigentlichem Wohnhaus, Gewächshaus und kleinem Gästetrakt – in den Kontext, stellte eine grosse planerische Herausforderung dar. Eine schon existierende mandelförmige Umfriedung, welche als Figur beibehalten wurde, gab die Grundrissform vor, ein grosses, intensiv begrüntes Betondach überspannt das gesamte Baufeld. An verschiedenen «Ausbissen» im Dach kann Landschaft in das Innere dringen. Darunter fädeln sich – einem präzisen Raumprogramm folgend – alle Räumlichkeiten auf drei Ebenen, einem Untergeschoss und zwei oberirdischen Geschossen, auf. Zwischen dem Wohntrakt und dem Gästehaus liegt das Gewächshaus, ein brückenartiger Schwimmkanal verbindet die beiden Gebäudeteile. Der topografische Anspruch versucht die in früherer Zeit abgeflachte Hügelkuppe wieder herzustellen, während sich das Gebäude von seiner typologischen Seite an die grossen Landhäuser aus der jüngeren und älteren Vergangenheit orientiert.

The winning project for an international invitation project combines the building's topographical and typological demands. Inserting this considerable volume – an ensemble of the actual home, a greenhouse and a small guest wing – into the context proved to be a considerable planning challenge. An already existing, almond-shaped surrounding wall, which was retained as a figure, dictated the ground plan's form. A large concrete roof with intensive greenery covers the entire building site. At various "outcrops" in the roof, the landscape penetrates the building. Beneath it, all the rooms on the three levels follow a precise spatial programme, interweaving with each other on the basement and the two overground levels. The greenhouse is situated between the living section and the guest wing. A bridge-like swimming channel connects the two building sections. The topographic intention attempts to restore the brow of the hill, which was flattened in earlier times, while typologically, the building is orientated towards grand country homes, both recent and from the more distant past.

Werkverzeichnis / List of Works

Auswahl Bauten, Projekte, Wettbewerbe und Ausstellungen
Selection of buildings, projects, competitions and exhibitions

1992		Wettbewerb Neues Messeareal, Bozen, IT
1993		Landesausstellung *Eines Fürsten Traum*, Schloss Tirol, Dorf Tirol, IT
1994		Wettbewerb Erweiterung EURAC, Bozen, IT
1998		Lagerturm, Weingut Hofstätter, Tramin, IT
1999		Josefsburg, Festung Kufstein, Kufstein, AT
2000		Landesausstellung *De Ludo Globi*, Brixen, IT
		Landesbergbaumuseum, Steinhaus, Ahrntal, IT
	1	Friedensbrücke, Kaltern, IT
2002		Dorfgestaltung und Lichtkonzept, Kaltern, IT
		Umbau Schloss Tirol, Dorf Tirol, IT
		Restaurierung Ruine Laimburg, Pfatten, IT
		Pharmaziemuseum, Brixen, IT
		Umbau, Haus Marktplatz 6, Kaltern, IT
2003		Arbeiterhaus Graf Enzenberg, Terlan, IT
		Territoriales Leitsystem «wein.kaltern», Kaltern, IT
2004		Weingut Manincor, Kaltern, IT
2005		Wettbewerb Evangelische Christuskirche, Innsbruck, AT
	2	Bar zum lustigen Krokodil, Kaltern, IT
2006	3	Barriquekeller, Kellerei St. Michael Eppan, Eppan, IT
		Wechselausstellung Landesjagdmuseum Schloss Wolfsthurn, Ridnaun, IT
		Wettbewerb Erweiterung Museum Joanneum, Graz, AT
2007		Bar ett?, Bruneck, IT
		Projekt Weingut Tenuta Ampeleia, Roccatederighi, IT
		Projekt Bürohaus Holzbau Damiani, Brixen, IT
		Wettbewerb Uferbebauung Mondello, Palermo, IT
		Wohnung R, Girlan, IT
2008		Eingangspavillion Gretl am See, Kaltern, IT
		Vinothek, Weingut Hofstätter, Tramin, IT
		Projekt Umbau und Erweiterung, Villa Salmi / van Riemsdijk, Arezzo, IT

1 2

2008 Sparkasse, Kaltern, IT
Wettbewerb Erschliessung Bergamo Alta, Bergamo, IT
Projekt Restaurierung Chateau la Motte, Arvier, IT
Projekt Pavillon, Lajen, IT
Projekt Wohnhaus für Tuchfabrik Moessmer, Bruneck, IT
2009 Besucherzentrum Karersee, Welschnofen, IT
Projekt Neue Kellerei, Meran, IT
Umbau Dachgeschoss Remichhof, Kaltern, IT
Raststation Lanz, Natz-Schabs, IT
Wettbewerb Erweiterung Hauptschule, Rattenberg, AT
Wettbewerb Erweiterung Zoo, Frankfurt, DE
Wettbewerb Beleuchtungskonzept, Hall i. T., AT; 1. Preis
Gewächshaus Ansitz Drescher, Kaltern, IT
2010 Umbau «Stadel», Ansitz Manincor, Kaltern, IT
Erweiterung und Sanierung Grundschule, Neumarkt, IT
Vinothek der Kellerei St. Michael Eppan, Eppan, IT
4 Flagshipstore Tuchfabrik Moessmer, Bozen, IT
2011 Dachausbau Ansitz Tonvin, Kaltern, IT
Projekt Weingut Tenuta la Torre, Velletri, IT
5 Ausstellung *Amol eppas ondorsch*, Innsbruck, AT
Projekt Versuchsgärtnerei Psenner, Girlan, IT
Haus V, Kaltern, IT
Wettbewerb Areal Oberer Stadtplatz, Kufstein, AT
Sammlerhaus D, Bozen, IT
2012 Wettbewerb Schwarzensteinhütte, St. Johann (Ahrntal), IT
Umbau Haus Mayer-Rieckh, Innsbruck, AT
Projekt Foyer Landhaus 1, Bozen, IT
Projekt Dorfgestaltung, Neumarkt, IT
2013 Wettbewerb Wohnbebauung Kirchenwirt, Innsbruck, AT
Wettbewerb Parkhaus Longea, Moena, IT
Haus T, Eppan, IT
Konzeptstore Oberrauch Zitt, Bozen, IT

3

4

2013 Adaptierung Haus S, Kaltern, IT
Projekt Ansitz Greifenburg, Kaltern, IT
Projekt Aussichtsplattform Biotop Kalterersee, Kaltern, IT
2014 Interventionen, Schloss Tirol, Dorf Tirol, IT
Haus Prey, Neumarkt, IT
6 Büroeinrichtung Südtiroler Marketing Gesellschaft, Bozen, IT
Hofstelle St. Quirinus, Kaltern, IT
Wettbewerb St. Michaelskapelle, Kirche Mariahilf, Bregenz, AT
Wettbewerb Eisstadion, Bruneck, IT
Projektstudie zum «Piffraderrelief», Bozen, IT
Projekt Stadtentwicklungskonzepte für Furth im Walde, Waldmünchen, Rötz, DE
2015 Projekt Erweiterung Haus G, Kaltern, IT
Tor Ansitz Drescher, Kaltern, IT
Wettbewerb Umgestaltung der Kirche am Ölrain, Bregenz, AT
Wettbewerb Mahnmal Euthanasieopfer, Hall i. T., AT; 1. Preis
Feldhütte im Weinberg, Kaltern, IT
Pressesaal der Südtiroler Landesregierung, Bozen, IT
Wettbewerb Erweiterung der Fachschule für Metall, Innsbruck, AT
Projekt Erweiterung Erste + Neue Kellerei, Kaltern, IT
2016 Weingut Thomas Pichler, Kaltern, IT
Wettbewerb Dorfzentrum und Bürgerhaus, Redwitz, DE
Projekt Tinne Museum, Klausen, IT

Laufende Projekte / Current projects
Restaurierung und Adaptierung Hospiz St. Florian, Neumarkt, IT
Neue Bibliothek, Kaltern, IT
Umbau und Erweiterung Maurarcherhof, Bozen, IT
Restaurierung und Adaptierung der Wickenburg, Eppan, IT
Adaptierung und Erweiterung Haus VW, Kaltern, IT
Adaptierung und Neues Badehaus Seehotel Ambach, Kaltern, IT
Wohnhaus K, Eppan, IT
Landhaus D, Dornbirn, AT

5

6

Nachrede

Arno Ritter*

«Bauen mit Hausverstand ist eine Mischung aus Pragmatismus, Programmatik und kultureller Reflexion. Das Streben nach einer verantwortungsbewussten Weiterentwicklung genügt meist.»
Walter Angonese

Walter Angonese ist einer jener Architekten, die ohne Einsicht in ihre Herkunft, Biografie und Lebensweise nicht ganz zu verstehen sind, da sich aus diesem biografischen «Gewölle» ein Teil ihrer kreativen Leidenschaft speist. Im Weindorf Kaltern geboren, wollte er ursprünglich Önologe werden, landete aber für zwei Jahre im Landesdenkmalamt von Südtirol und studierte gleichzeitig in Venedig Architektur. Diese biografischen Umwege markieren jene zentralen Themenfelder, zwischen denen er sich architektonisch bewegt: Geschichte, Landschaft und Alltag. Es ist seine Auseinandersetzung mit der Topografie, dem historischen Kontext und den Alltagsgeschichten vor Ort, die massgeblich die Bauten prägen. Als treuer Bürger am «Endchen der Welt» und zwischen den Welten, verwoben mit den internationalen Entwicklungen in Kunst und Architektur, agiert er aus jener ambivalenten Haltung heraus, die zwischen dem Provinziellen und Globalen pendelt und diese Spannung als Grundlage des Denkens von Architektur empfindet. Seine permanente Suche nach konzeptioneller Klarheit wie gestalterischer Verortung verdichtet sich für ihn im Begriff des Weiterbauens, der als Leitmotiv seiner Entwurfsmethodik zu verstehen ist. In seiner Auffassung ist alles Bauen eigentlich Weiterbauen, denn Architektur bedeutet für ihn, das Vorhandene als Grundlage des Entwurfs zu nehmen; zuerst die einzelnen Schichten der Konventionen freizulegen, die Geschichte wie deren Verwerfungen zu befragen und infrage zu stellen; sich mit kulturellen, gesellschaftlichen wie sozialen Bedingungen der Aufgabenstellung auseinanderzusetzen, um auf Basis dieser Erkenntnisse eigenständige Lösungen zu generieren, die auf den ersten Blick manchmal unscheinbar, oft aber auch markant sind, und immer wieder irritieren, weil sie zu nah und doch zu fern der Konvention oder dem architektonischen Zeitgeist liegen. Denn Walter Angonese hat keine Berührungsängste mit einfachen, scheinbar banalen Lösungen und orientiert sich am anonymen Bauen, das die Pragmatik des Alltags zu gestalten versucht. Nicht selten spielt er in seinen Projekten mit Elementen der architektonischen Hochsprache und der Mundart des Bauens, kombiniert oft unterschiedliche Bedeutungsebenen von Material

* *Arno Ritter* wurde 1965 in Wien geboren. Er studierte Publizistik, Geschichte und Philosophie an der Universität Wien. Von 1992 bis 1995 war er Sekretär der ÖGFA – Österreichische Gesellschaft für Architektur. Seit 1995 leitet und programmiert er den Ausstellungsraum «aut. architektur und tirol» in Innsbruck (vormals Architekturforum Tirol), den er als Ort der Präsentation von Architektur, Kunst, Design und Grafik sowie als Raum der interdisziplinären Diskussion über die Gestaltung unseres Lebensraumes positionierte. Seit 1999 ist er Mitglied des Landeskulturbeirates für Tirol, war von 2000 bis 2005 Vorstandsmitglied der Architekturstiftung Österreich und von 2005 bis 2009 Mitglied des Beirats «Kunst und Bau» des Landes Vorarlberg. An der Universität Innsbruck hatte er von 2003 bis 2012 einen Lehrauftrag für Architekturkritik sowie Kuratorische Praxis und war 2009/10 Lehrbeauftragter an der Universität für Angewandte Kunst in Wien am Institut für «Transmediale Kunst». 2012 war er Kommissär des österreichischen Beitrages auf der Architekturbiennale in Venedig und ist seit 2015 mit Peter Zumthor Beirat des Werkraums Bregenzerwald. Als Herausgeber und Autor publiziert er vorwiegend zu Architektur, Fotografie und Kunst.

Afterword

Arno Ritter*

"Building with common sense is a mixture of pragmatism, programme and cultural reflection. Striving for responsible further development is mostly sufficient."
Walter Angonese

Walter Angonese is one of those architects who cannot be fully understood without knowing their origins, biographies and lifestyles, since part of their creative passion draws from their biographical background. Born in the wine-making village of Caldaro, he originally intended to become a oenologist, but ended up in the State Monument Preservation Office of South Tyrol for two years and simultaneously studied Architecture in Venice. Such biographical detours define central themes between which he moves architecturally: history, landscape and everyday life. It is his examination of the topography, the historical context and the everyday stories at the location that has a definitive influence on the buildings. As a loyal citizen of the "little corner of the world" and existing between worlds, combined with an awareness of international developments in art and architecture, he operates with an ambivalent stance that oscillates between the provincial and the global, since he considers tension to form the basis of architectural thinking. His permanent search for conceptual clarity and design localisation is concentrated in the term of continued building, which can be regarded as a guiding principle of his design methods. From his perspective, all building is really continued building, since he believes in taking existing structures as the basis of the design, initially revealing the individual layers of the conventions, to investigate and question the location's history and its mutations, to study the cultural and social conditions of the task, and to generate independent solutions based on that insight, ones that may initially appear inconspicuous, but are often also striking and repeatedly irritating, because they come too close to and yet move too far away from the architectural zeitgeist. Walter Angonese has no problems with simple, apparently banal solutions and is orientated towards anonymous building that attempts to design the pragmatism of everyday life. In his architectural projects, he regularly plays with elements of standard architectural language and the dialect of building, often combining different levels of significance with respect to material and form, thereby achieving an ambivalence that is surprising and unconventional. In that sense, Walter Angonese not only uses bricks and concrete as a

* *Arno Ritter* was born in Vienna in 1965. He studied Journalism, History and Philosophy at the University of Vienna. From 1992 to 1995, he was Secretary of ÖGFA – Österreichische Gesellschaft für Architektur. Since 1995, he has managed and curated the exhibition space "aut. architektur und tirol" in Innsbruck (formerly Architekturforum Tirol), which he has positioned as a space for interdisciplinary discussion on designing our living environment. Since 1999, he has been a member of the State Cultural Advisory Committee for Tirol, was a Board Member of the Architekturstiftung Österreich from 2000 to 2005, and was a member of the State of Vorarlberg's "Kunst und Bau" Committee from 2005 to 2009. From 2003 to 2012, he taught Architectural Criticism and Practical Curating at the University of Innsbruck. From 2009 to 2010, he was a Lecturer at the University of Applied Arts Vienna at the Institute for "Transmedial Art". In 2012 he was Commissioner of the Austrian contribution to the Architecture Biennale in Venice and since 2015 has joined Peter Zumthor on the Committee of the Werkraum Bregenzerwald. The journalist and author mainly publishes on architecture, photography and art.

wie Form und schafft damit eine Mehrdeutigkeit, die überrascht und unkonventionell ist. In diesem Sinne verwendet Walter Angonese als «Baumaterial» nicht nur Ziegel und Beton, sondern auch das Wort, da er im Dialog mit den Bauherren, den Handwerkern und seinen Partnern die Projekte auch sprachlich entwickelt und im Prozess spontan antwortet.

Im positiven Sinne könnte man Walter Angonese als Eklektiker bezeichnen, da er aus Büchern, aus der Welt der Kunst und Architektur wie des anonymen Bauens, auf seinen Reisen und durch seine Professur in Mendrisio ständig Themen, Bilder, Konzepte und formale Lösungen aufsaugt, diese sich setzen lässt, um zu gegebenem Anlass aus dieser dichten «Nährflüssigkeit» seine kreativen Energien zu beziehen. Oft entwickelt er Projekte im Dialog mit befreundeten Architekten oder Künstlern, viele mit Manfred Alois Mayr, mit dem ein symbiotisches Reibungsverhältnis über die Jahre entstanden ist, das von den beiden als «kreatives Blödeln» bezeichnet wird. Ihr verfeinertes Reiz-Reaktions-Verhältnis spiegelt auch die Fotografie am Anfang des Buches wider, die von Manfred Alois Mayr spontan auf das Buchkonzept in Rom entstanden ist. Aus diesem Wechselspiel der kreativen Kräfte entstanden Bauten, in denen nicht mehr nachvollziehbar ist, wo die Architektur beginnt und die künstlerische Intervention aufhört beziehungsweise wer was wo entschieden hat. Im fast schon wörtlichen Sinn reden die Bauten von Walter Angonese in unterschiedlichen Sprachen, verhalten sich zumeist leicht ironisch zu sich und dem Kontext, was letztlich ihre konzeptionelle wie formale Unverwechselbarkeit ausmacht.

"building material", but also words, since in dialogue with the client, craftsmen and his partners, he also develops the projects verbally and finds spontaneous answers to them in the process.

One could describe Walter Angonese as an eclectic in the positive sense of the word, since he constantly absorbs themes, images, concepts and formal solutions from the worlds of art, architecture and anonymous building, as well as on his travels and through his Professorship in Mendrisio, allowing them to settle before drawing his creative energy from that condensed "nutrient fluid" at the appropriate occasion. Often he develops projects in dialogue with befriended architects and artists, many together with Manfred Alois Mayr, with whom a symbiotic frictional relationship has developed over the years, one that both describe as "creative fooling around". Their refined relationship of stimulus and reaction is also reflected in the photography at the beginning of the book, which was conceived spontaneously by Manfred Alois Mayr in Rome as a reaction to the book concept. Such interaction between creative forces has produced buildings where it is no longer visible where the architecture begins and the artistic intervention ends, in other words who decided what and where. Almost literally, the buildings by Walter Angonese speak in different languages, mostly behaving in a slightly ironic manner with respect to the context, which ultimately defines their conceptual and formal unmistakability.

Walter Angonese

1961	geboren in Kaltern, IT
1980–1983	Studium der Agrarwissenschaften in Bologna, IT
1983–1990	Architekturstudium IUAV, Venezia, IT (Diplom bei Vittorio Gregotti)
1990–1992	Mitarbeiter beim Landesdenkmalamt Südtirol, Bozen, IT
1992	Gründung des Büros a5 angonese scherer galvagnini architekten, Bozen, IT
1999–2000	Lehrauftrag für Entwerfen, Universität Innsbruck, AT
2002	Gründung des eigenen Architekturbüros, Kaltern, IT
seit 2005	Mitglied des Kollegiums für Landschaftsschutz der Autonomen Provinz Bozen, Südtirol
2007–2011	Gastprofessur an der Accademia di Architettura in Mendrisio, CH
seit 2011	Ordentlicher Professor für Architektur an der Accademia di Architettura in Mendrisio, CH
2012–2015	Mitglied des Gestaltungsbeirates der Stadt Salzburg, AT
seit 2015	Vorsitzender des Gestaltungsbeirates der Stadt Salzburg, AT
seit 1998	Vortragender und Gastkritiker an den Universitäten von Palermo, Reggio Calabria, Napoli, Roma, Cagliari, Genova, Torino, Milano, Venezia, Innsbruck, Graz, Wien, München, Stuttgart, Bamberg, Aachen, Berlin, Vaduz, Zürich, Winterthur, Grenoble, Delft, Porto, Viseu, Sevilla, London etc.

1961	Born in Caldaro, IT
1980–1983	Studied Agriculture in Bologna, IT
1983–1990	Studied Architecture at the IUAV, Venezia, IT (Diploma under Vittorio Gregotti)
1990–1992	Employed at the South Tyrol State Monument Office, Bolzano, IT
1992	Founded the office a5 angonese scherer galvagnini architekten, Bolzano, IT
1999–2000	Lecturer in Design, University of Innsbruck, AT
2002	Founded his own architectural office in Caldaro, IT
since 2005	Member of the College of Landscape Protection for the Autonomous Province of Bolzano, South Tyrol
2007–2011	Guest Professor at the Academy of Architecture in Mendrisio, CH
since 2011	Professor ordinarius of Architecture at the Academy of Architecture in Mendrisio, CH
2012–2015	Member of the Advisory Board for Urban Design of the City of Salzburg, AT
since 2015	Chairman of the Advisory Board for Urban Design of the City of Salzburg, AT
since 1998	Lecturer and guest critic at the universities in Palermo, Reggio Calabria, Napoli, Roma, Cagliari, Genova, Torino, Milano, Venice, Innsbruck, Graz, Vienna, Munich, Stuttgart, Bamberg, Aachen, Berlin, Vaduz, Zurich, Winterthur, Grenoble, Delft, Porto, Viseu, Seville, London etc.

ProjektpartnerInnen / Project partners

artec architekten (Bettina Goetz, Richard Manahl), Maria Auböck + Janos Káráz, Axel Beck, Paolo Belloni, Ingenieurteam Bergmeister, bergmeisterwolf architekten (Gerd Bergmeister, Michaela Wolf), Corrado Binel, Eduardo Cappuccio, Carola Daldoss, Nicola Di Battista, Giuseppe Donato, Manfred Draxl, Andreas Egger, Florio Faccendi, Elena Galvagnini, CN10 architetti (Gianluca Gelmini, Andrea Pressiani), Giner + Wucherer (Thomas Giner, Erich Wucherer), Klaus Hellweger, Rainer Köberl, Armin Lahner, Hansjörg Letzner, Herbert Mair, Andrea Marastoni, Manfred Alois Mayr, Vincenzo Melluso, Mario Monotti, Wolfgang Piller, Markus Scherer, Kathrin Schiefer, Paul Senoner, Thomas Tschöll, Sandro Vasari, Susanne Waiz

MitarbeiterInnen/Employees seit/since 2000

Sanja Balta Radic, Silvia Boday, Filippo Bolognese, Alessia Carlotto, Maria Dissertori, Magdalena Donà, Francesco Flaim, Mortiz Gaiser, Theo Gallmetzer, Christoph Gapp, Alfred Gufler, Kathrin Hofer, Olaf Koehler, Katrin Lahner, Eva Mair, Matthias Mair, Esther March, Andrea Mazzucotelli, Martin Pertoll, Silvia Potente, Haimo Prünster, Quirin Prünster, Manfred Rauch, Rendervalley (Federico Testa), Kathrin Schiefer, Martin Trebo, Thomas Tschöll, Jacopo Vantini, VG13 (Tommaso Fantini, Alberto Rossi, Emilio Trevisol), Lukas Wielander

ÁLVARO SIZA
SAMSUNG

Bibliografie/Bibliography
(Auswahl/Selection of)

Casabella Nr. 726/2004
Almanacco 1998
Identità Italiana 2014/2015
Architektur Aktuell Nr. 236/1999, 242/2000, 249/2000, 291/2004, 373/2011, 384/2012, 402/2013, 435/2016
Architese Nr. 03/2004, 05/2013
Modulor Nr. 05/2011
Domus Nr. 932/2010, 989/2015
Domus (deutsche Ausgabe) Nr. 16/2016
Architektur und Bauforum Nr. 209/2000
Baumeister Nr. 12/2004, 11/2006
d'Architettura Nr. 31/2006
Bauwelt Nr. 35/2006
Baunetz Nr. 439/2016
de Architetectura Nr. 21/2009
Oris Nr. 56/2009
Turris Babel Nr. 89/2012, 91/2012, 93/2013, 96/2014, 06/2015
Neue Zürcher Zeitung Nr. 282/2005, 199/2013
Ottagono Nr. 244/2011
Zuschnitt Nr. 45/2012
mark Nr. 42/2013
a10 Nr. 51/2013
the plan Nr. 65/2013
archi Nr. 04/2012
flash art Nr. 297/2014
exibart Nr. 09/2014
Manincor. Neuer Weinkeller. Schlebrügge 2005
WeinArchitektur (Katalog). Hatje Canz 2005
Residential Buildings as Motivation. Fourre-Tout/Götz 2008
Wohn Raum Alpen (Buch). Birkhäuser 2010
Architektur & Wein (Buch). Callwey 2010
Auf Gebautem bauen (Buch). Folio 2005
Neues Bauen in den Alpen (Buch). Birkhäuser 2008
heimat bauen. Klemmm & Oelschläger 2009
Architektur in Südtirol (Buch). Callwey 2008
Kunst in Tirol (Buch). Tyrolia 2007
Mein liebster Stuhl (Buch). Callwey 2008
Wein + Raum (Buch). Detail 2014
«Ernst A. Plischke Preis 2014». Müry Salzmann 2014

Eigene Textbeiträge in/Articles by Walter Angonese
Singular Plural GD Architects. Birkhäuser 2012
Idea and Concept. Niggli 2012
Museen in Tirol und Südtirol. Athesia 2009
Village Textures. Schlebrügge 2014
Die Kunst des Flickens. Brunnenburg 2014
Arte Hotel Bregaglia, das Kunstereignis. Hier und Jetzt 2014
Neues Leben in alten Mauern. Athesia 2011
Weiterbauen am Lande. Studienverlag 2014
L'Atlante dell'Architetto / The Architect's Atlas. MAP/SilvanaEditoriale 2016

Finanzielle und ideelle Unterstützung / Financial and conceptual support

Ein besonderer Dank gilt den Sponsorfirmen, deren finanzielle Unterstützungen wesentlich zum Entstehen dieser Buchreihe beitragen.
Ihr kulturelles Engagement ermöglicht ein fruchtbares und freundschaftliches Zusammenwirken von Baukultur und Bauwirtschaft.

auroport *doors and gates, www.auroport.it*

barth *building interior architecture, www.barth.it*

fischnaller *steel and glass, www.fischnaller.info*

Quart Verlag Luzern / Quart Publishers Lucerne

De aedibus international

14 Walter Angonese (de/en)
13 architecten de vydler vinck taillieu (de/en)
12 De Smet Vermeulen architecten (de/en, nl/fr)
11 Uwe Schröder (de/en)
10 Stephen Taylor Architects (de/en)
9 Titus Bernhard Architekten (de/en)
8 Dietrich|Untertrifaller (de/en)
7 Geurst & Schulze Architecten (de/en)
6 Wingender Hovenier Architecten (de/en)
5 Tony Fretton Architects (de/en)
4 Jonathan Woolf Architects (de/en)
3 Hufnagel Pütz Rafaelian (de/en)
2 Hild und K (de/en)
1 Stanton Williams (de/en)

Monografien/Monographs

koepflipartner – landschaftsarchitekten / landscape architects (de/en)
Graber & Steiger. Bauten und Projekte 1995–2015 (de)
Vincent Mangeat. Logos & Faber (de/en/fr)
Sergison Bates architects (de und en)
Peter Kunz. Bauten (de/en)
Miroslav Šik. Architektur 1988–2012 (de/en)
Valerio Olgiati (de und en)
Burkard Meyer. Konkret/Concrete (de/en)
Gion A. Caminada. Cul zuffel e l'aura dado (de/en)
Bearth & Deplazes. Konstrukte/Constructs (de/en; vergriffen / out of stock)

Quart Verlag GmbH, Heinz Wirz; Verlag für Architektur und Kunst
Denkmalstrasse 2, CH-6006 Luzern; books@quart.ch, www.quart.ch